BOD

DAD
BOD

DAD
BOD

portraits of
pop culture
papas

CIAN CRUISE

RARE
MACHINES

Epigraphs on page 125 from Joseph Campbell's *The Masks of God: Creative Mythology*, Digital Edition, Copyright 2016 © Joseph Campbell Foundation (jcf.org). Used with permission.

Publisher: Scott Fraser | Acquiring editor: Julie Mannell
Cover designer: Laura Boyle
Cover image: suit: istock.com/VasjaKoman tshirt: istock.com/AaronAmat

Library and Archives Canada Cataloguing in Publication

Title: Dad bod : portraits of pop culture papas / Cian Cruise.
Names: Cruise, Cian, author.
Identifiers: Canadiana (print) 20220165416 | Canadiana (ebook) 20220165440 |
  ISBN 9781459749474 (softcover) | ISBN 9781459749481 (PDF) | ISBN 9781459749498
  (EPUB)
Subjects: LCSH: Fathers. | LCSH: Fatherhood. | LCSH: Fathers in mass media. |
  LCSH: Men in popular culture.
Classification: LCC HQ756 .C78 2022 | DDC 306.874/2—dc23

We acknowledge the support of the Canada Council for the Arts and the Ontario Arts Council for our publishing program. We also acknowledge the financial support of the Government of Ontario, through the Ontario Book Publishing Tax Credit and Ontario Creates, and the Government of Canada.

Printed and bound in Canada.

Rare Machines, an imprint of Dundurn Press
1382 Queen Street East
Toronto, Ontario, Canada M4L 1C9
dundurn.com, @dundurnpress 𝕐 f ⌾

For my family

Contents

Prologue

What is a man? A miserable little pile of secrets.
— Dracula, *Castlevania: Symphony of the Night*, "Prologue"

ON THE EVENING OF DECEMBER 21, 2018, I was standing in the stone cold of a polar vortex outside of my local rep cinema, The Revue. I was with my brothers- and sisters-in-law, but not my wife. She was almost a week overdue, and her family had come up to Toronto so that we could spend some time together for the holidays. This was the last movie I would see before my son was born, four days later, after thirty-six hours of labour, at two thirty in the afternoon on Christmas Day.

We were waiting in line to see *Die Hard*.

It is shocking, in retrospect, how appropriate it was that *Die Hard* was the last movie I saw before becoming a dad. *Die Hard* has been, for many, many years, my deeply avowed favourite film. I've seen *Die Hard* in theatres over twenty times. I've seen it on television, monitors, and airplanes countless more. Each time I am in the presence of Bruce Willis's greatest contribution to the human condition, a rictus grin of pure unadulterated entertainment is plastered on my face.

When I was twelve, my grandmother bought me the *Die Hard* trilogy on VHS. It came in a gunmetal-grey box that weighed as much as my approaching adolescence. This movie shaped me in many weird ways. I developed a bizarre habit of always looking for hiding spots when I entered a new place,[1] *just in case* terrorists (who weren't really terrorists) struck, so that I could be the one person not caught by them and could thus disrupt their nefarious plans. The fly in the ointment. The monkey in the wrench.

During university, I studied film, which meant that I watched a lot of movies that were nothing like *Die Hard*. And yet, even my art-house Iranian film professor made us watch *Die Hard* to analyze its script and pacing. This woman devoted an entire lecture to how bad she thought *The Big Lebowski* was. Just hated it. The films she made were weird, artisanal vlogs from a pre-YouTube time. Diarist entrails of a purely esoteric artistic aristocracy. And yet, *even she* said that *Die Hard* was "a Swiss watch of a film." Every structural element of the plot beat with perfect precision.

Now, as I continue to study the craft of writing, and I look back on *Die Hard*, I find myself surprised by the weird layers it has, and what it can tell us about family, masculinity, and the action-movie genre itself.[2]

But none of that was on my mind on December 21, 2018. I just wanted to watch my favourite movie with some new people, and relieve a bit of the tension that came from waiting for my overdue baby to be born.

•

---

1. School, arena, friend's house, mall.
2. We'll get to all that later, trust me.

Two weeks later, my wife and I were on the couch, bingeing the first two seasons of the *Castlevania*[1] animated series on Netflix.[2]

My wife was propped up with pillows, recovering from the visceral ordeal of childbirth. She was akin to a warrior of old, resting after a duel with the forces of nature. Like Beowulf, she was filled with old-fashioned Germanic mirth after her brush with both the cosmic and the chthonic. She had brought new life from within her out into the world. Our son. Our little god. A miracle emerging from the kiln of chaos.

Knees up, legs apart, ice applied at regular intervals.

On her laptop, Dracula was in an old-fashioned punchout with his son, Alucard. They had cast aside weapons and magic, allies and pretense, stripped down to the eternal power struggle between father and son. Expressed in that most primal form of violence, the fist.

We were riveted to our tiny screen as Dracula repeatedly slugged his dhampir son through the thick stone walls of the Count's Gothic castle complex.

Then Dracula punched Alucard through one last wall, into Alucard's childhood bedroom.

And something amazing happened.

The high-octane, excellently animated battle set piece dissolved into a broken monologue — and for six or seven

---

1. *Castlevania* video games have been in my life even longer than *Die Hard*. My thumbs first blessed a Belmont's whip at the tender age of seven, at before-school care, with a pack of kids huddled around an old CRT monitor, swapping the controller with each death. I was the only one who made it past Stage 1. By the time I scraped my way to Stage 3 (basking in the glittering awe of my peers) and the opening chiptune organ smashes of "Wicked Child" (YouTube it) — dodging flying Medusa heads and killer ravens — I was hooked. Everything about it: the over-the-top Gothic style, the nonsensical action, the difficulty that rewarded memorization and dexterity, the magic flaming whip, the monsters — I was in seven-year-old heaven.

2. This was exactly two years ago, as I write this. (Three years, as I edit it.)

seconds, *Castlevania* transcended its genre, medium, and franchise history.[1]

Upon seeing his son's nursery, the superhuman rage bled out of Dracula's eyes. "My boy," Dracula said, taloned hands clutching his chest. "I'm killing my boy."

Those two words messed us up. They were delivered with such authenticity and skill, I have to call out Graham McTavish's vocal chords. Magnificent pipes. Between shared tears, my wife and I looked over at our son, sleeping in his little motorized swing set.

"We painted this room, we made these toys," Dracula continued, soliloquizing now to his dead wife. "It's our boy. Your greatest gift to me, and I'm killing him." He paused.

"I must already be dead."

The Lord of Darkness mourning his lost child — and, through it, his own lost humanity — was a hot emotional knife neither of us was prepared for. We had signed up for a spot of adventure and undead slaying to get us through the afternoon, not inadvertent profundity.

On the surface, *Castlevania* is about fighting werewolves and vampires with a magic whip. Just beneath that shape-shifting skin, it's a story about family. Broken families, lost families, the families we make ourselves out of the ashes of our lives, and pain. Real pain wrapped up in phantasy and starfire.

Then, back in the show, with excruciating deliberation, Alucard slides a wooden stake[2] into his own father. The

---

1. Like, it's a series of video games about a clan of vampire hunters who train their entire lives on the off chance that Dracula is resurrected and that his magic castle emerges from the mist, spewing demons into the land. Then one of them goes to the castle and murders their way through the demons, right into the throat of the castle, and whips Dracula back to death. Yes, the family has a magic whip that passes down from generation to generation. It is the only thing that can subdue Dracula. *Hamlet* this is not.

2. A piece of his broken childhood bed, no less!

world-ending crisis[1] is averted and the machine of plot grinds on, leaving in its wake this moment of absurd sublimity to two new parents, so exhausted that they will take wisdom in the shape of fangs and magic and monsters.

Because when you have a kid, everything becomes profound. Everything they do. Everything you witness. Everything your new family experiences is the first time it has ever happened in the universe, and it comes with an emotional avalanche that hits even harder than Dracula's left hook.

Between these two scenes, bookended by these two pillars of pop culture that loom large in the media mausoleum of my consciousness, my life changed forever — my entire identity changed in ways that will continue to unfold for the rest of my life.

I became a father.

There is a little human being that my wife and I are responsible for. We're responsible for his life. His upbringing. His safety. His world view.

He calls me "Daddy." And when I look into his eyes, I see the cosmos.[2]

Everything is completely different now. My life is totally different. And yet, I am still the exact same knucklehead. I still love *Die Hard*. I still think too much about *Castlevania*. I naively assumed that, when I became a father, something would change within me to help me become a better person. But I'm still the same guy, only sleep-deprived and overwhelmed by new emotions and frequently in the presence of a little person who arrests my attention so utterly it's like the sun has crept into the room.

---

1. Because there's always a world-ending crisis, am I right?
2. Fun fact: my dad wanted to name me "Cosmo Cruise."

Change, if it has happened, is subtle. Or else I'm oblivious. There's an incredible paradox with many experiences of growth. I never feel further from change than when it is imminent. During that visit with her family, my wife was dead certain our son would never be born. Instead, he would continue to gestate within her massive stomach for eternity. She had been pregnant for so long, her entire body and spirit subsumed into the process, it became impossible to remember a time when she wasn't pregnant.

Our whole world was pregnancy. How could that change?

The unknown was inconceivable.

And then it happened.

PART ONE:
Foundations

By Way of Introduction

You must have a little patience. I have undertaken, you see, to write not only my life, but my opinions also; hoping and expecting that your knowledge of my character, and what kind of a mortal I am, by the one, would give you a better relish of the other: As you proceed further with me, the slight acquaintance which is now beginning betwixt us, will grow into familiarity; and that, unless one of us is at fault, will terminate in friendship.... Therefore, my dear friend and companion ... if I should seem now and then to trifle upon the road, — or should sometimes put on a fool's cap with a bell to it, for a moment or two as we pass along, — don't fly off, — but rather courteously give me credit for a little more wisdom than appears upon my outside; — and as we jogg on, either laugh with me, or at me, or in short, do any thing, — only keep your temper.

— Laurence Sterne, *The Life and Opinions of Tristram Shandy, Gentleman*[1]

---

1. Although I straight up stole this from the epigraph of Dave Hickey's excellent essay collection *Air Guitar*.

I HAVE THE HARDEST TIME writing about myself. Generally speaking, the non-fiction I write is about film, television, and video games. In these essays, I bury and obfuscate myself in good-time-Charlie-style analysis. I see my role as somewhat like a teppanyaki chef, slicing and dicing interesting bits and pieces then flipping them into your mouth in the tastiest order. "I" am not the focus, something else is. At most, I'm an interesting lens through which you, the reader, can experience a cool perspective on some new ideas. A good lens is invisible, and shouldn't bring too much attention to itself, even as it inevitably warps the subject of consideration.

Otherwise, it's a bit like a scalpel trying to cut itself. If·I analyze and describe my own experiences too directly, I become an ouroboros of intestinal articulation. The feedback loop of self-dissecting-self results in a thick layer of snowy noise.

That's why I'm starting with *Die Hard* and *Castlevania*. With quotes from *Tristram Shandy*. That's a big part of the reason why I'm going to try to talk about what it is like for me to become a father — that shift of identity and the deepest understanding of one's role in the world — through the locus of a bunch of goofy shows and games. It helps me hide, so that I can say something real. But it also helps me find a touchstone, a point of departure, that we might share.

By the same token, these cultural products matter a great deal to me. I am invested in these works of mass media entertainment fiction to a dubious degree. Even if I'm not explicitly aiming my lens of analysis at myself, I am on the line here. I care about stories way, way too much. So even though this is an oblique entranceway, I am still opening the door and trying to welcome you into my weird, labyrinthine heart.[1]

---

1. Which is also a mystery *to me*! Were I to attempt a direct and explicit articulation, it would be a lie!

For better or worse, my sense of self is informed by these many pieces of art that I spend the majority of my waking life contemplating. In a way, diving deep into these texts *is* getting to know me a heckuva lot better than narrative biographical detail.

That doesn't mean I'll be entirely absent, some detached voice claiming ethereal authority. Like I said, I'm *in* this. I am a new dad, after all. My hope to understand what it means to become a father in our day and age — what it means to me, and what it means to others — is a wholly internally driven enterprise.

.

Which brings us to the "dad bod." It's high time I start to unpack that one.

The term initially popped up in 2015, as an example of the curious media sphere we currently live in. Mackenzie Pearson, a student at the time, coined the term in her college newspaper, claiming that a guy who was less-than-ripped was actually *more* attractive.[1]

Pearson provided a tight psychological argument: a guy with a dad bod is sort of in shape, but doesn't take it too seriously; that means a guy with a dad bod is less self-obsessed; he therefore has good priorities; and being *with* a guy with a dad bod doesn't make a woman feel bad about her own body, given society's ever-crushing mandate to make women undermine their self-worth at every opportunity.

Always starved for content, newspapers of record, magazines, websites, blogs, Twitterers, YouTubers, and late-night talk show hosts glommed on to this new term and ran with it, until it entered our cultural lexicon.

---

1. Mackenzie Pearson, "Why Girls Love the Dad Bod," *The Odyssey*, March 30, 2015.

Then, five years later, science caught up with a sophomore's intuitions.[1] Researchers found that women associated the dad bod with all kinds of incredible parenting behaviours,[2] and they rated the "toned gym bod" the absolute dog's breakfast. They thought cut men were trash. If they wanted a fling, sure, they'd go for some jacked torpedo, but when it came to making a real life together, the dad bod won out.

(I should of course mention that the "dad bod" male body used in the study is better understood as "Hollywood-casual dad bod," as opposed to the bodies of actual real people. Think Jon Hamm in *Mad Men*, not Seth Rogen in anything.)

This is where things get interesting.

The fact that these researchers could so easily populate a study with the exact same psychological assertions found in a college newspaper's initial hot take indicates that there is something going on here. It seems like folks really are making these deep associations based on the image and perception of male physique.

Of course, it's hogwash. But it's very interesting hogwash. Our illusions tell us as much, or perhaps even more, about us as our truths.

The dad bod is an acceptance that images, and particularly media-driven images of fatherhood, are essential to our knee-jerk apparatus for navigating the world. When push comes to shove and we are bombarded with imagery all the dang day long, we will fall back upon the associations and patterns that Occam's razor provides, regardless of how well they stand up to sober scrutiny.

---

1. Donald F. Sacco et al., "Dad and Mom Bods? Inferences of Parenting Ability from Bodily Cues," *Evolutionary Psychological Science* 6, no. 3 (September 2020): 207–14.

2. Like, "Babies melt this person's heart," or "This person tries to teach their children new things." From their physique alone! With no faces, even!

This association is also an acceptance — within that image, and only to a certain extent — of "softness" within the definition of mass-marketable masculinity. Specifically, the softening that accompanies placing other people's needs before your own. That softening might not be a bad thing, despite dudes' initial reluctance to accept it.[1] Constant attention upon the self is unsustainable. If you temper steel repeatedly, it becomes brittle. If you question and re-question your motivations, you become an anxious, paralyzed mess. If you focus on yourself to the exclusion of others, you become a narcissistic monster. This sounds a lot like a recipe for toxic masculinity!

So maybe "softness" is great. Let's be honest, masculinity needs all kinds of help, especially when it comes to identity and definition.[2] A centuries-long Spartan obsession with hardness and toughness and pseudo-military ethos in entirely inappropriate circumstances, combined with an utter disregard for emotional intelligence and sensitivity, has not served men well. Softness can undo that, or at least provide the beginnings for approaching a different way of being a man.[3]

Lastly, this peculiar bundle of associations illustrates the dynamic exchange between culture and self as art imitates life imitating art (that's playing at life (while watching art (between episodes of living life))).

•

---

1. I know it's been hard for me. I was never cut, but I was in shape. I ran, and I did rock climbing. I was lithe. Now I'm not. And even though I have a very hard time with the way my body has changed post-fatherhood, my wife finds the "thickness" alluring.

2. In some way, shape, or form that isn't exclusionary or bigoted.

3. Not that this is the first time someone's tried to redefine masculinity. Nor is this the only avenue for change. Hardly. It's one potentially interesting crack in the brittle armour of old man tough guy.

I see culture as a soup, and we're swimming in it. (No, that's not a mixed metaphor.) Unless you are some kind of hermit, you are inundated with carefully curated images day in and day out. Both carefully curated by you for self-selected need and interest, but also carefully curated by whomever is trying to make a buck off your attention.

"Fatherhood," as a cultural concept, is one such current in the broader bowl of masculinity, which is, itself, balanced on an island of mushy crackers called "identity." And though these elements are ever in flux, a relational web between all the things we see and hear, all the art we imbibe, and all the conversations we have nestles in our mind like worms. Among all that froth and bother, relatively coherent nets of meaning float to the surface, and keep bobbing up and down in our psyche, no matter how many times we push them back down into the broth.

What I'm saying is: every single dad that I have ever seen in a TV show or movie helped inform my idea of fatherhood. Those images are burned indelibly into my mind's retina, albeit vaguely, whether I want them or not. They inhabit a similar space as my friends' dads growing up. They did not raise me, I have but a broken picture of them both, but I have a total feel for their vibe.

It is key to discuss the vague, flabby shape that these dad bods have as cultural figures.[1] What presence they exert independent of the text, the constellation of associations that these figures exert in shorthand.

We know these dads. By the very fact of their cultural presence, they exist like mind-worms haunting the souls of all the people that you know. In the same way grandparents who are like, "You never gave your daughter Barbies, but now she's

---

1. Or chunks of gristle in our cultural soup.

totally into Barbies, SEE? GENDER IS REAL," are not being
very good detectives[1] — that daughter just came in contact
with the culture mind-worm that's infected every other child
in her school, a hive as large and wide as the entire media ecosystem, sowing its spores wherever screens emit their liquid
crystal dreams.

So, to take the temperature of these mind-worms, I want
to write as descriptive a subjective analysis as I can, to try and
capture one data point: How do these dad-figures seem, to me,
glimmering and warbling in the distorted breeze of my nostalgia-
and-caffeine-soaked brain? What is the gist that they give off,
such that we would tap into an informal conversation with a
co-worker or lesser-known acquaintance, when we don't have
access to the fact-checking apparatus of the internet? Because it
is this gyre of accreted half-truths that makes up our gut take on
so many things. Our fundamental understanding of fatherhood
is no different.

Like I said above, this swirling panoply of figures of fatherhood — these dad bods — act in a similar way as the fathers of
my friends growing up. I very much *don't* have the experience
of being raised by them, even though I've witnessed examples
of their style of fathering. I witnessed their spirit, and that tells
us so much about what it means to be a father. Until we have
the Matrix and can download an entire life of experiences into
our noodle, the closest thing that we have are the distilled ex-
trapolations rendered in the process of creating popular fiction.

In part, this is because there is no guidebook for being You
as a parent. You are you. Your kid is your kid. There are too
many granular variables. And yet, that vibe speaks volumes.
You see it between the moments of action, in the gestalt of
being a dad. That's what we're looking at here, and we're going

---

1. Poirot would be ashamed of this premature deduction.

to have to peer deep and in between sunbursts of gross incandescence to find that midnight sun from which our shadowy image of fatherhood spawns.

I'm not here to critique art, not really, but rather to dissect the dads portrayed within, and describe what it unveils to me as a person trying to figure out what it means to be a dad — to be *me* as a dad — in the present moment, by comparing these archetypes and examples that permeate our culture.

•

Another way of putting it is to ask, "What story has the media been trying to sell me about fatherhood?"

As I noted above, this isn't something that I have any choice in. We all swim in our culture's soup. We don't get to choose what "orthodox" is; all we can do is try to see it, and figure out if that's how we want to live. That requires distance, and curiosity. So my process is one of distanciation: an attempt to look at the tropes and archetypes inside me as though I'm an outsider, which requires absorbing as many alternative perspectives as possible — via these works of art — and using them like a crowbar to lever my assumptions and, hopefully, reveal what's beneath them. I have to try to break it down like an alien would, unaware of connections that seem obvious to us,[1] all the while balancing the dual mind, the alien and the insider, the critic and the memoirist, because, well, otherwise it would be gibberish.[2]

So I'm balancing as best I can. Seeing from both perspectives simultaneously to attempt to manifest a binocular vision.

---

1. Or like an intellectual yokel, asking honestly dumb questions to see where it takes us.

2. Bear in mind, this thing is written after being drunk on sleep deprivation for two years. Take these pieces of text not as "writing," per se, so much as howls that have echoed their way from the depths of my soul. Either because they scream with the most clarity, or the most immanence, or because I'm sleepwalking.

Take two, relatively two-dimensional pictures of what it means to be/become a father and, by arranging a composite of both, render a new, three-dimensional image.

Undoubtedly, I will slip every now and again, falling off one side or the other on this balance beam. It's those moments of awkwardness when I ask for a bit of forbearance. I'm going to try and keep the momentum up, so that when I slip off that tightrope, it won't be for too long, and, by reaching one arm up, over the other side, I can (hopefully) flip back up and keep this whole edifice hopping, skipping, and jumping along.

Or I'll fall flat on my face, and at least we can share a laugh.

404 Dad Not Found

EVERY DAD STARTS WITH A pregnant lady.[1] Hell, every *person* starts with a pregnant lady, at least until we can rig up those birthing pods. After my wife gave birth, I wandered around the city in a permanent haze of wonder. In part because of sleep deprivation, but in part because it was absolutely incredible to think about the fact that each and every person's mother went through some variation of the incredible, epic journey of giving birth. Every mother we talked to had an incredible birth story. It's impossible to look at folks emptying out of the subway and not be riveted in utter awe at the miraculous process through which each of their mothers carried them, nourished them in their bodies — grew them — and gave birth to them.

It's overwhelming when it's just your kid. Then you realize that this happened to each and every one of us, and the raw magic of reality shimmers along the surface of all humanity.

In fact, I can't believe that there isn't an entire genre of films about pregnancy and supporting your pregnant wife/partner. It should be bigger than rom-coms. This is easily one of the most

---

1. Twice.

relatable stories out there. It has literally the best happy ending
you could possibly imagine,[1] one that would flood the brains of
every parent in the audience with uncontrollable joy chemicals.

I mean, heck, every time I watch some random movie that
even contains babies in it, I lose my saline. My wife and I were
watching a documentary about a couple who started organic
farming. Ninety-nine percent of this thing is about how much
of a problem coyotes and gophers and bugs and birds and grass
are, right, then ten minutes from the end they're like, "Oh
yeah, by the way, we had a kid" — and BOOM there's this
little boy traipsing around the farm, making friends with their
puppies and pigs in his cute overalls, and I'm balling over here
because I don't see that little kid. When they show the wife
pregnantly farming, I don't see her. When she's in labour and
they have to use a vet or something, I don't see her childbirth.

In my heart, I see my kid. I see my wife. I see our son's
birth. I relive it all, that entire year condensed into an emotion-
diamond, each facet blindingly bright.

This started happening just a few weeks after I became a
dad: I transformed into a total sucker for any and all marketing
efforts aimed at me via the vector of babies and parenting. You
show me an ad about chocolate or cars or life insurance, and as
long as there's a baby or a little kid in there, I am emotionally
engaged. My chest swells, my nose quivers, and my tear ducts
assume the ready position.

I can't help it. And I'm trained not to care about ads. My
first real job out of university was writing advertisements just
like this. My brain analyzes copy based on theoretical frame-
works of engagement and use of visual space. And yet, that is
no defence when your heart has been can-opened up by the act
of becoming a parent.

------

1. Or the most devastatingly sad ending.

I can't imagine that this feeling goes away as my child ages. In fact, the farther away babyhood becomes, the more precious those images are. While the remembrance of my wife's trek through the mountains of pregnancy and the gauntlet of child-birth transcends reporting and enters the echoing halls of myth.

So imagine, instead of a thirty-second ad spot about wiping up spilled juice, an entire Hollywood manifestation — engineered for perfect, efficient emotional manipulation, bearing down upon the open soul of the newly forged mothers and fathers of the world.

And yet this is a gaping hole in our media tapestry.

If you need a ready-made bite-sized indictment against the sexism interwoven into our[1] culture like a quarter-helix of its DNA (the other bits being white supremacy, capitalism, colonialism, cosmopolitanism, and Christianity), then look no further. I mean, if I phrased this entire inquiry slightly differently — "Why isn't pregnancy/childbirth a major dramatic genre?" — my wife and female friends give me a one-word answer: "Sexism." And they're right! But by playing the straight man here,[2] we can see what this lack means, what it does, and what it tells us about ourselves as a people — in addition to the fact that our mainstream culture is straight-up sexist.

When our mainstream entertainment menu features a thousand flavours of "Muscleman punches and drives an exploding car," but only a handful of "Solid guy grows up a bit," and an utter dearth of "Woman has a meaningful life experience," it does something to our culture. It spices that soup, so to speak, and we slurp it down. It establishes a criterion for

---

1. North American, that is. If you are reading this from Europe, Africa, Asia, or South America: Hi! I didn't expect you, but thanks for showing up! The reason I want to use the possessive pronoun here is to take ownership of this sexism. It's a part of me, whether I like it or not.

2. And elsewhere.

what counts as "entertainment," which in turn informs what it means to be a person, what stories are worth telling, and what life events are meaningful.

I want to explore that lack. These telling absences indicate what we're being sold about the image of fatherhood just as much as the emphasized archetypes, albeit in relief. The fact that it starts with pregnancy is too poetic for me to resist.

1. You aren't the main character anymore, man.

This is the big one that I really dug about being a man supporting my wife during her pregnancy and childbirth. It became very clear that my role was subsumed within hers. I, a white guy, who has mostly been told that I am the centre of my particular universe, needed to learn how to be there for someone else. Not in the way I thought they needed to be supported, but in the way that they actually needed to be supported.

A great example from our childbirth class reared its head on the big day: No Questions. Delivering a child is a very psychological experience. A mother-to-be needs to be in the zone for birth to proceed. Even *thinking* about answering a nervous husband's questions[1] takes her out of her body and into an abstract space. For that matter, asking those questions implies a re-centring of emotional attention[2] on the father-to-be: tell me what to do, comfort my lack of understanding, provide leadership for me, guide me.

Me. Me. Me. Me. Me.

No way, man. You gotta anticipate. You gotta empathize. You gotta figure out what that mom needs, as she needs it. Before she needs it.

---

1. "What do you want?" — "What do you need?" — "Is there anything I can help with?"

2. And labour.

This is an incredibly valuable life skill, and it's totally bonkers that it isn't taught (generally, culturally) to men ... ever. We're barely taught to be cognizant of our own emotional needs, and instead tend to perceive emotions[1] as a swirl of indistinct colours with external reasons that only become named when we dump them all over other people who are forced to put up with our bullshit.

By sublimating this trend, and learning to see how to put another person first, a new father gets to prototype a microcosm of parenting — in other words: of the rest of their life. Your kid's needs are more important than yours. Without this essential intuition, you become one of those weird general-dads who uses kids to further their own agenda, the dark inversion of which is living vicariously through your kid's achievements. In both, the kids aren't people. They are mere props to your identity.

If, on the other hand, we had a genre of movies that were derived from the need to learn how to put oneself definitively second for nine months, and learn how to perceive others in a way that acknowledges their emotional reality and anticipates their needs, it would go a long way toward providing a rough framework for the kind of emotional and individual growth that most men my age are deprived of due to overwhelming cultural pressure to be "The Hero" (and the myriad manifestations that moniker demarcates) rather than a human being.

And you know what? Those could be some darn entertaining movies. I am very bad at not asking questions in moments of duress. I want a lot of clarity before I act. A guy like me

---

1. When we even do. Given the history of men being psychological bilge pumps enacting an infantile, hydraulic model of emotions that smoulders somewhere between a toddler and the Incredible Hulk, "perception" might be too advanced a term. Emotions surprise men. Emotions assault men. We have no words, and thus we sink in a sea of invisible internal forces.

learning how to support his pregnant wife (on my own, not asking my wife to "train" me, not getting hints from the midwives) was a kung-fu comedy's worth of hijinks,[1] and I can only imagine that if you multiply the basic archetypes of guys by the basic archetypes of gals, mix in a few LGBTQ+ couples, toss an overbearing parent or two in, and you could have all manner of plotlines that all end in the biggest gosh darn climax of a person's life.

Now *that's* cinema.

2. However, pregnancy is coded as a dramatic imposition, not a complete "story."

Oh boy. This one really burns my bridges.[2] Part of my research for this essay was attempting to see just what movies were out there that portrayed pregnancy as a central plot point, in the hopes that I'd be caught flat-footed by one. No such luck.

The main pregnancy plotlines are

a. high-powered executive woman has surprise baby and succumbs to natural instincts;

b. teen gets pregnant by mistake, learns to deal with it in a probably heartwarming fashion; and

c. a pair of adults have a one-night stand, resulting in an unwanted pregnancy that plays out like (a) + (b) but also love guides the way.

Heck, the biggest outliers I could find were *Junior*, for crying out loud,[3] and *What to Expect When You're Expecting*, which is based on a textbook.

---

1. I did an objectively "okay" job, and I still nearly drowned my wife in orange juice after she delivered our son.

2. Not my britches. What I mean is: I can't stop seeing this. I can't go back to my previous ignorant bliss.

3. Which is just plot (a) with Arnold Schwarzenegger, A SCIENTIST MAN, as the career-focused "mother."

See the common thread? When it is central to a plot, pregnancy is coded as a dramatic imposition, as a problem that gets the story going, and must be overcome, or dealt with, or embraced. It isn't the goal. It doesn't factor in to anyone's plans. It's the hoary breath of Poseidon knocking your ship asunder.

Supporting your wife throughout pregnancy doesn't qualify as a story due to the structural elements that film scripts rely on for their very existence. Or, to be a bit less extreme: a narrative of this nature demands far more subtlety in establishing a new kind of structure than our current examples, all of which try to shoehorn pregnancy into an existing comedy sub-genre.

Let's break it down. Drama hinges on conflict. The bigger the better. The more physical and external, the easier it is to film and the less you have to rely on subtext and multi-dimensional dialogue.

In terms of basic structure, film relies on an interruption to the status quo and the quest to right it. The only change involved is bound up in the protagonist, more or less, and it neatly coincides with the source of conflict. Everything, and I mean everything, ought to tie in to this central conflict. That's what makes it a story.

When you try to introduce pregnancy into that framework, it gets a little weird, because having a kid is a tectonic shift that alters the landscape of two[1] lives irrevocably. It is some *Book of Genesis*–level reordering. Entire worlds, selves, and perspectives explode in a cascading array of newfound senses and sensibilities.

It is a simultaneously subtle and blunt-force-trauma obvious experience. A screaming, blood-covered spawn erupts from your genitals and, like the Grinch, your heart grows three sizes.

------

1. Or one. Or a dozen!

But it isn't the same as the "inciting event" that a script needs, because it usually isn't a problem.

That's why the vast majority of films about pregnancy are about unwanted pregnancies. They're about coping with that big surprise, growing to incorporate this new need, realizing that, even though you're a hard-as-nails corporate woman with a harem of hot executive lovers, you too can discover the milk of mother's kindness.

In these paint-by-numbers movies, pregnancy is an imposition. It's a disruption to the status quo. In real life,[1] I'd like to posit that pregnancy, and supporting your pregnant wife, is a quest in and of itself. One that demands incredible growth and development to undertake in an intentional, earnest, healthy, sane way. And one that continues far after the climax.[2]

This is perhaps obvious, but it is also not apparent in any of the successful movies about pregnancy that I trenched through with the same grim mien that accompanies four o'clock wake-ups and my toddler's near-constant demand for Saturday morning cartoons. Instead, they all focus on a sliding scale of: lost opportunities, unprepared idiots, and teenagers. At best they end on mystical platitudes where brain chemicals provide the *deus ex machina* and a calorie-free fairy-tale ending.[3]

What this utter lack of dramatic attention on the pregnant experience implies is that it isn't important. It isn't even a story. It's not worth investing with the needs drama asks of us: bringing our entire heart and mind to the picture.

Instead, pregnancy and childbirth are relegated to the role of mere plot devices.

---

1. And the genre I wished existed.

2. Both of them.

3. Even Arnold is guilty of this in *Junior*. Everything just sort of magically works out and they frolic on a beach.

3. Men aren't "naturally" capable of parenting.

This is pernicious as all get-out. Even in an ostensibly — what's three notches down from "woke"? Not quite progressive. Maybe paper-tiger progressive? Centrist? Wait, now I've got it: even in an ostensibly "modern" romantic comedy featuring pregnancy, *What to Expect When You're Expecting*, the assumption is that men start from a disadvantage when it comes to child-rearing compared to women — a *natural, inborn* disadvantage — which is centre ring in the whole problem-circus that I'm wrangling here.

There's an unspoken assumption riven throughout our culture that men don't or shouldn't care about babies, or about the act of caregiving. Plenty of men do anyway, but supposedly they're few and far between.

So when a movie comes along like *What to Expect*,[1] which you can tell is kind of trying to mildly upend some stereotypes of masculine care, but in order to do so, has to first pander to those stereotypes so as not to alienate the target audience, it gets awful weird awful fast and — even worse — I would say it gets mired in that initial assumption set and holds fast. In part that's because of the preceding two points. The movie still has to be "about" the man's journey, rather than the complex of a newly forming family,[2] and the pregnancy must still be dramatically coded as an imposition.

What's worse, the film is five vignettes about pregnancy shoved into a phone booth, giving none of them the opportunity to delve deeper than a pamphlet.

In the main plotline, instead of an executive badass lady becoming un-jaded, now the imposition is "This guy needs to be taught what fatherhood is really all about" (by Chris Rock, I

---

1. I refuse to type out the rest of the title again.
2. Or, you know, the pregnant woman.

guess, and some other "regular guys"[1] from a token-filled group of market-research demography), because this pregnancy imposition is *happening to him*.

Throughout, we learn that it is okay to buy a lot of child-rearing paraphernalia, and that you can still "be a real man" based on your previous straw-thin definition *and* have a baby around but not, really, take care of it in any tangible way. The idea here is that these guys are advanced because they are willing to spend time being seen in public with their babies. This is like a guy who expects a standing ovation for deigning to do the dishes. They high-five about low expectations and a lack of judgment upon one another's fundamental discomfort and awkwardness around children, revealing that the way forward is, basically, a kind of neutered apathy that is considered a vast improvement over top of the initial starting place of emotional, logistical, and domestic incompetence.

It honestly feels like the script was written by the kind of guy who gets the heebie-jeebies by accidentally walking into the women's section of a department store.

As always, the book is better than the movie.

.

Okay, so all roads lead to sexism, after all. I should've listened to the women in my life, once again. How has there been so little progress in such a long amount of time? What are the mechanics of this assumption-laden fantasy of ignoramus fathers, that gets men off the hook from continuing to develop as people past the age of eighteen?

For that, I'm going to have to turn to Ted Danson, as I often do in times of duress.

.

---

1. Wait, are they *all* stand-up comedians?

Three Men and a Baby plays off the exact same comedic stereotypes of *What to Expect*, and the movie was released in 1987.
That's a twenty-five-year gap. It's the kind of movie I might've
seen when I was a kid, and only half-understood what was
going on as I peered between my parents' knees on a Sunday
afternoon, face hidden behind a pillow when they told me a
"grown-up" scene was coming.

For a quick refresher, *Three Men* is about three eligible
bachelors, played by Ted Danson, Tom Selleck, and Steve
Guttenberg, and directed by Spock,[1] of all people. One day, a
baby shows up on their doorstep, product of a tryst one of them
had. They are utterly incompetent caregivers, but they fall in
love with the child while simultaneously dealing with some
heroin dealers, because you've gotta have a plot. Their landlady
teaches them how to take care of the baby, and eventually the
baby's mother shows up to first fight, then join them.

The three key stereotypes about babies and men are right
there: the men are the main characters, the baby's a narrative
imposition, and guys are naturally hopeless when it comes to
care.

In two and a half decades, the needle of basic cultural assumptions about masculinity and child-rearing from *Three
Men and a Baby* to *What to Expect When You're Expecting*
moved exactly bupkis.

The value of looking at *Three Men* is that it shows us
how men get off the hook: we tend to judge men as we would
boys. Never mind the fact that these characters are profes-
sionals (an actor, an architect, and a cartoonist), they are
boys, living in a kind of super-clubhouse apartment complex.
Their main concern at the beginning of the film is partying.

---

1. Leonard Nimoy will always be Spock to me, despite the fact that his first autobio-
graphy was titled *I Am Not Spock* and dealt, in part, with the actor's identity crisis
following *Star Trek*'s overwhelming popularity.

Period. Tom Selleck was forty-two when this flick came out, and we're led to believe that his character wanted nothing more but a carefree life of booze, babes, and bacon. Have you ever met a forty-two-year-old architect? All the ones I know fall straight into the category of board-game players, if you catch my drift. Catan and seltzer on a Wednesday night, not rum and Coke.

.

Anyway, the initial disparity is clear — guys don't know shit about being parents. The thing is, nobody does. This crazy assumption that somehow women have an inborn talent for nurturing is the boldest slice of propaganda since Mao's Five-Year Plan. They learn it. They bother to pay attention. They don't have a choice, you see, because the baby is there, as raw a reality as you can muster, and they just have to figure it out (given that the men in our culture have convinced themselves that they can't even learn — *inborn, innit?* — and convinced everyone else that they don't have to — thanks, patriarchy!). If the women hadn't stepped up to the plate for the past few thousand years, we'd be doing a hell of a lot worse as a species.

And, because these cockamamie assumptions make it so difficult to make material contrary to the market research of Hollywood's overseers, we're all so much more impoverished and misaligned.

Pregnancy happens offstage. Men become dads with no ritual or education. Then they grow up, and remain boys forever. Dads around the world believe that they have to fight against an inborn inability to be empathetic, nurturing caregivers. Society passes that meme on from generation to generation.

And we end up in a place where it seems sensible to base a reading of a man's emotional capabilities on the thick lipid wall of his torso, rather than, I don't know, pretending like you could have an adult conversation about his interior landscape.

A world where everyone judges a book by its cover.

A culture full of dad bods, but bereft of father figures.

Foreword, Afterword, Side-to-Sideword

IF YOU ARE LOOKING FOR some brass-tacks life lessons about being a dad, this is not the book for you. This is a series of essays that attempt to build a conceptual vocabulary about the idea of fatherhood as it is portrayed through a bunch of media that *also* paint a life story. A bit like an amateur[1] anthropologist, I'm going to walk through the Venn diagram of (a) the stories that have resonated with my core, the kind that hit a bell that's still ringing in the back of my mind ten, twenty, thirty years later, combined with (b) stories that tell us something about the external shape and assumptions of fatherhood as it is portrayed in commercial entertainment. That story we're being sold of what it means to be a dad.

Having said all that, I do want to let you in on some of the secrets of dadhood. After thinking about *What to Expect When You're Expecting*, the premise of that guidebook franchise is basically "there are all of these crazy details about being pregnant that you will not find out until it is too late not to have

---

1. And very narrowly focused.

a kid," albeit told in a schoolmarm patronizing kind of way. That's all well and good, and if I had my druthers, books like it would be way more explicit, way more fun, and way more revealing.

One of the most important lessons you learn when you're reading books and taking classes about pregnancy is that your story is going to be utterly idiosyncratic. Nobody else is going to have a pregnancy or a birth quite like yours. One of our pieces of homework from prenatal class was to go and talk to four different mothers about their birth stories, and they were all over the map. The take-home was twofold: yours, too, will be unique, *and* it will be unpredictable. Get rid of the idea you have in your head about the kind of birth story that you want, because it is maximally unlikely that it is going to go down that way, unless you book yourself in for an induction/C-section.[1]

Going through that disillusion is great training for parenthood, because being a parent is also not going to be anything like what you expect it to be.

Even though I can't really talk about global trends in parenting science, I do want to share some of the constants that have emerged from talking to the dads I know. Now that I'm on the other side and have a little life spawn hanging out with me, there is an unspoken code between me and any other father, with a child at any life stage, and that bond is forged instantaneously.

I wouldn't exactly call it a "brotherhood," as this isn't a support network and we aren't helping each other out. It's more like the public-facing side of a mystery cult from ancient Rome. We can see the signs that someone has been initiated into the

---

1. Which only reduces the variables, rather than removing them. That savvy kid might come out a week early! Or any number of surprises may arise post-induction. Booking a C-section might be more predictable, but not necessarily.

mysteries of fatherhood, and the way they weather the seas of dadship are writ plain on their face. If you don't know what I'm talking about, just hang around a playground sometime,[1] until you see two lone dads interact. In fact, for the best possible chances of seeing more than one lone dad with their child at the park, go on a Saturday or Sunday morning. Statistically,[2] that's when dads take their kids to the park solo.

Wait until the dads have a reason to interact. They probably won't talk unless they already know each other, but they will for sure check each other out. When they make eye contact, that's when you'll see it. The exchange of information that goes both above and below language. They might not even nod. They don't need to nod. They both know, even though they don't know how, exactly what the other has gone through to get there, and if they have any sensitivity at all, they respect that.

Picture two grizzled veterans from two different wars sharing a drink. They get each other wordlessly. Or that old Zen saying, "When two Zen masters meet on the road, they need no introduction. Thieves recognize one another instantaneously."

What do they know? Let me tell you all about that first flight of fatherhood.

1. 60 percent is your new limit.

You will never be at your best. Maybe you'll get there once your kid is past the toddler years, but those first four years are going to be rough. A marathon of masochism. Have you ever worked a few years without proper sleep? If not, welcome to a whole new hell. It's like there is a constant white noise happening in the base of your skull, right where the pineal gland

---

1. Do so wisely, especially you single men in the audience. There are all kinds of problematic vibes a single dude at a playground gives off. Sorry not sorry, other parents will label you a threat no matter what you do or do not do.

2. Or at least anecdotally.

connects to the noumenal world. You can never quite hear it, never quite not hear it. A sort of psychic tinnitus, this constant mental instability means that you are going to be able to handle about 60 percent of the things that you used to be able to. Good luck.

I wish to the old gods someone had put it in these terms for me.

Instead, people say stuff like, "Oh, you'll have less time for yourself." Which totally varnishes over the part where you will have less time and also your brain will be melting out your ears because remembering how to make a cheese sandwich took up all of your available mental cycles and the laundry still needs to be done and you can totally forget about reading a book before bedtime as you will find yourself reading the same paragraph over and over, unsure whether or not your mind is processing the words or merely running over top of them like a child runs over top of one of those rubber slat bridges at the playground and did I remember to unpack the wet clothes from L—'s bag after we went to the park, because if I don't we might not go into that bag for another week and his shirt might grow fungus like that super cute one with the bear on it that we had to throw out because the stain that we thought was chocolate milk was actually mould.

So: prepare yourself for being less than capable. Warn the people in your life. Especially for the first three months, which are an otherworldly journey like Dante's *Inferno* without Virgil to help you through the rough parts, but also the next few years. People are willing to bring you lasagna and soba for those first three months, which is awesome,[1] don't get me wrong, but unless you are the kind of person who is lucky enough to live within some sort of commune complex with your extended

---

1. Thanks, Sean and Yumi!

family,[1] that support will shrivel up, and then you'll have to go back to work and do your job to an adequate level and remember how to take care of yourself and try, desperately, to hold onto some iota of the picture that you have of yourself in your head and where you want to go in life, rather than succumb entirely to the role of parent.

2. Your kid is the biggest thing.

I don't mean this symbolically, not really. When your kid steps into the room, they will seem bigger, brighter, than anyone or anything else. You won't be able to help but notice them. A significant chunk of your mental bandwidth will vanish every time your child enters the room. A great example is the "is there a knife on the top of the counter" phase of learning how to walk, but it isn't just explicit worries or dangers that trigger this other kind of fog from the sleep-deprivation one mentioned above.

Your kid will seem bigger than other kids who are the exact same size. Your kid will seem smarter. They will seem cooler. More fun. More beautiful. All of those subjective measures that contribute to parents thinking the objectively inaccurate things they do about their progeny is spurred on by this raw chunk of magnetic attention.

The first time this became obvious to me, my wife and I were trying to share Thanksgiving in the park with some of our friends who we hadn't seen much in the first ten months of our son's life. Since we didn't have time to cook, we'd bought about $150 worth of Swiss Chalet and packed it up the night before (in our one-bedroom apartment, silently, as our son slept) in coolers and carry cases. When we set out the spread and sat

---

1. In which case you probably don't need to read these kinds of descriptions because you already know: you're surrounded by people having kids and can see for your damn self.

around with the handful of folks we wanted to catch up with — I had nothing to say.

As I'm sure you can guess already, despite our relatively new relationship here between these pages, "not having something to say" isn't an affliction that occurs too regularly to me.

Thankfully, these friends all knew each other and were able to carry on a conversation as I helped make sure that our son didn't wander off from the picnic blankets or ingest a bottle cap or any of the other shenanigans a ten-month-old will get up to.

Then my wife took L— for a swim in the nearby city pool.

The instant they were out of eyesight, boom, the gates sprang open and my mind[1] returned to me. The division was stunning in its lucidity. I was back, baby! I could riff and keep up with my friends, which had been an impossible task mere moments before. It's like the difference between being sick or healthy,[2] except that the change-up is instantaneous.

My wife experiences the inverse. Whenever she gets into a social situation that demands greater than average attention or engagement, she finds that it overrides the part of her brain that is ambiently aware of our son's goings-on. She seems to only be able to enter into this state when in a space that she knows is baby-proofed, but the switch-up is still palpable. She doesn't have any more control over it than I do, but it happens in the opposite direction — right up until our son makes a noise, or is quiet for too long, or something happens in another room. Then she snaps back into risk assessment and action, her voice reaching out to comfort and soothe, her attention attenuated to his direct and applicable needs.

---

1. Or at least 60 percent of it.

2. Or having a headache and, well, not having a headache.

3. Never cool again.

I went to a farm today with my kid. A theme park farm. A place where they had play tractors strewn around in a sand-filled pit, and a series of playgrounds made up like outbuildings and barns, the entire area bordered by goats. The website said they had horses, alpacas, sheep, and donkeys, but all I saw was an army of goats. Kids ran around pell-mell from one welded-in-place farm implement to another.

Nobody was cool there. It was impossible to be cool there.

That's parenthood. "Cool" is no longer a value. If you depend upon it for self-esteem, I am so, so sorry. If you try to stay cool when your kid is asking you to climb aboard a retrofitted lawn tractor and hit the buttons, here's what you're going to do: Remain aloof. Not join in. Leave them to their own devices.

That is some cranky ass Victorian shit. No, you're going to get in there, if your heart isn't carved from granite. And you're going to love it. And it isn't going to be cool and you will discover[1] that that's okay.

It's freeing.

4. You are always, always on.

I've never had a job where I'm on call, so I was really not ready for this one. There is no "off," when it comes to day-to-day parenting. There are times when your partner is taking care of the kid, or when the kid is in daycare, but generally those are times when you are doing something else, like work, which is hardly "time off."

In fact, I remember discussing parental guilty pleasures with my barber, who has a child a year older than mine. The big one we shared: getting groceries. Going out on an errand

---

1. Similar to what I discovered once I was in a committed relationship: I could go to a party without the anxiety of "whether or not I'd meet someone," and, instead, could just focus on having a good time with the people I knew and the people I met.

by myself felt like playing hooky, for all of the bandwidth and time and attention reasons noted above: when you are alone is the closest you are going to get to time off for the next little while.

Other than that hour every once in a while, you are always on. Your kid is right there, watching what you do, absorbing your mannerisms and your words, absorbing the interactions that you have with the people around you, absorbing every little thing that you do or do not do out in the world. Sometimes it feels a bit like being in a stage play. As an actor onstage, you have to be aware of every aspect of your body and your voice, while you attempt to inhabit a certain persona and project it out into the world. I remember an old stage adage that you should always remain in character for about ten feet offstage, otherwise (if you only aim to maintain the character until you hit the curtain) folks might see the disassembling as you ease back into your self each step of the way, shattering the drama's illusion.

Now, maybe you are the kind of person who has no personas (or thinks you don't) and you feel/believe that you act the same way in every single context. Maybe that's the case. Maybe you are the one-in-a-billion person who is not swayed by the social circumstances and perceived dynamics going on around you. You treat your dentist and your mother and your best friend exactly the same.

If you're like the rest of us, who talk one way to our boss and another way to our sisters, you're going to be putting on some kind of a character for your kid. Even if it is something as mild as not swearing, reprogramming your amplifying adjectives takes effort.

Some percentage of that persona will be conscious, some percentage unconscious, but it will be there. You as "Dad" versus you, alone in a room.

The thing is, you have to remember to take those ten extra feet to maintain the double-awareness that comes from being someone's parent. Otherwise, when the emotions hit the fan, the character will be stripped off, and it will be a jarring experience for all involved.

What's amazing is that the awareness that your kid is watching you isn't a burden, but rather an opportunity. There have been many times in my life when I had the ability to yank my consciousness out of the narrow track that it was chugging along and force myself to see me from a different angle. Having a kid is kind of like that, all the time.

They are always there, and as soon as they repeat something you say, out of the blue, then you start to grok the fact that they are always paying attention, which means that you need to be always on.

In my rough and ready morality, modelling a better person is being a better person, because what you do is the bottom line. By having this constant viewer, I'm taking more deep breaths when I feel my stress levels rising — because I want to teach L— to do the same. I'm controlling my inside voice — because I want L— to learn to do the same. I'm explaining my emotions more and more, which helps me understand them better and better — because I don't want L— to live in a miasma of tension and confusion like I do when it comes to my internal motivations and the way they spike out into the world. And I'm trying to dive straight into uncertainty, rather than follow my instincts to hold back and observe before trying out something new, even something as innocuous as a singalong circle group with other parents — because I want my son to be able to learn iteratively and not be controlled by the anxieties that haunt my brain.

None of that is easy. I have a lot of work to do as a person, a partner, and a dad. It doesn't feel easier because my son is watching me, but, now that I have that tug toward pseudo-objectivity, it feels *possible*. That's a start.

·

This book is a product of the above sketch of a person. I'm a new dad. I don't know what that means. I've spent a lot of time thinking about stories, and I want to burrow inside them like a sand flea to suck on the blood of our culture. At the same time, I don't trust myself, and I don't trust our popular culture, so I want to suck that blood to analyze and question its makeup, to distill the humours and the diseases within it, to the best of my individual ability, and act as one case study of a person trying to become a dad, and trying to become themselves, with the tools and the models that we have on hand.

Is it perfect? No, of course not. That's one of the first lessons you learn in parenting class, to give up the idea of perfection. On your birthing story, on your picture of what it'll be like to be a new parent, and on the idea that you can control your life.

Now a little person-worm will be in control. A wee emperor whose very life depends on your ability to toss aside perfection and instead get on with it.

·

This book was written within these conditions and limited capabilities. No time. No sleep. No sense of the bigger picture. A few, brief howls of clarity escaping from my bosom, and a bevy of dad bods clamouring in my mind's eye for attention.

PART TWO:

The Good, the Dad, and the Ugly

The Absent Heart of Robin Williams

FOR THE FIRST SIX MONTHS of my son's life, my wife and I were lucky enough to equally share most child-care duties. I was working flexible freelance hours from home, she was on maternity leave from her job as an executive director of an arts organization, and things were good. We lived in the kind of symbiotic harmony that only exists when two people intentionally decide to forego all other endeavours and focus their undivided attention upon a single, shared goal. But it couldn't last. The grim reality was that we needed more cold, hard cash to exist in this capitalist hellscape. So I scraped together a resumé and started the ancient rite of boasting about my deeds in the village square to secure a sinecure.

A few months later I was working three jobs: a nine-to-five sales manager position, some freelance consulting on the side, and writing whenever I could squeeze manna from the brittle stone of my soul.

It was terrible. I was working about fifteen hours a day, spending half an hour in the morning with my son in a sleep-deprived stupor,[1] and missing too many dinners and too many bedtimes to even pretend to be parenting anymore — or else racing home to get there on time, writing emails on the streetcar, writing emails in my head while tending to my son's needs, then writing emails deep into the night.

I kept it up for a year, and only left the nine-to-five job when Covid shut the world down.

My son grew *so much* in that time. I missed all of it. Even though I was "there"[2] for bits and pieces every day, I missed it because I was too blitzed out to be present. I was always thinking about something else, working on some problem, preparing a conversation in my head, or grimly enduring my quiet desperation with brute animal perseverance.

The thing is, I didn't realize just how much I had missed out on until, a few months into the pandemic, my wife and I sat up one night looking at family photos.

I didn't remember a single one. Each was a moment captured from a time I was not present, and that knowledge was a wolf chewing into my chest. I cried all night, mourning the son I still had, and the baby who was already becoming a toddler. I didn't know his weight in my arms, despite rocking him to sleep a hundred times.[3] I couldn't remember his smell. I hadn't been there for his first words, his first steps, his first glimmer of independence and autonomy and self.

Except for one moment, one clear crystallization of will made manifest.

On one of those terrible November mornings, as I prepared to march off to the streetcar after half an hour spent with my

---

1. I straight up forgot deodorant at least six times. I am so sorry, co-workers.

2. Quote unquote.

3. I used to bite my tongue and the inside of my mouth when I held him in the dark of night, because I read somewhere that pain helps a memory stick.

son while gobbling raisin toast and brushing my teeth, as I put my boots and coat on, my son had barricaded the door with his little body.

He'd had no words, at the time. All he could do was put himself between his father and the exit. All he knew how to do was sit between me and the place he did not want me to go. Away.

I want to say that I listened to the wordless plea of my baby. I want to say that I picked him up and held him in my arms and spent the day being a part of his life. I want to say I did the right thing.

Instead, I waited for his mother to distract him, as I stood there, dumbstruck and overwhelmed, burned out and hollow, too miserable to accept this too-human truth. Then I opened the door, kissed him goodbye, and went to work.

•

I know that I'm not special. That this pain isn't unique. It's a big part of being a parent, and, as one of my clients said when we were chatting, "This is one of the things that being a dad is all about. Not being there."

•

In the early '90s, everyone I knew wished Robin Williams was their dad. Not Robin Williams the person, because, let's be honest, only a handful of people had any idea who he really was. I mean the *idea* of Robin Williams, as propagated by his three central family-friendly roles: Peter Pan in *Hook*, the Genie in *Aladdin*, and the dad in *Mrs. Doubtfire*.[1]

---

1. Notice that I don't even name the character in *Mrs. Doubtfire*. I'm sure you've all seen *Mrs. Doubtfire*. Quick, without looking it up, what's his first name? Last name? Total blank. Doesn't matter. He isn't a real person. He's a mannequin that Mrs. Doubtfire can be draped upon.

Zany. Fun. Baroque. Touched by Dionysus. I had no male role models who even approximated the Robin Williams vibe.

And yet, on closer inspection, "fun" isn't what's really going on in these films. The persona we're being sold is the trailer version, the elevator pitch, and even though it is incredibly enticing to a ten-year-old who wants to eat ice cream and ride llamas to school while singing pirate shanties, this picture of fatherhood undermines the incredible loneliness at the core of Robin Williams's fathers — and the nightmare that having a dad like that would really be.

It's important to recall the essential absence that drives these films.

Left to his own devices, Peter Pan is a workaholic. He's so bad a father that his children find the well-known villain *of childhood itself,* Captain Hook, a suitable replacement. Sure, we're meant to surmise, by the film's end, that Peter's reformed and has discovered the true meaning of family. But it rings hollow. That revelation is only possible in the suspended reality of Neverland. It'll never actually happen. It's right in the name. This boy ain't gonna fly once we get back to the here and the now.

Once the fairy dust wears off[1] and vacation's over and he gets his cellphone back from that damn dog (I give him a week, tops), we'll be on a slow slide back to the beginning of the movie: missing recitals, late for ball games, making his children wish they were still hanging out with a taxidermy-obsessed pirate who at least gave them attention.

An intervention that depends on a magical world just can't last.

The Genie, of course, is a blood slave, not a father. He is Aladdin's dad only insofar as he provides a simulacrum of guidance. His continued existence relies on not pissing Aladdin off,

---

1. Read: cocaine. He's a lawyer in the '90s after all.

or countermanding Aladdin's dream wishes. There are dads like this, whose emotional equilibriums hinge on their kids' approval and thus invert the power dynamic. The Genie is like the dad who gives his kid a credit card and a car when they go to college and says, "Have fun." That dad proves an empty form of emotional support, as he provides no structure, boundaries, or discipline. In other words: only a fraction of the essential elements of parenting.

The Genie is a stand-in for the kind of guy who thinks that being a dad is all fun and games. Mom will handle the rest.[1] He builds an elaborate scaffolding of anti-logic about why he can't do the dishes, in essence playing on the fear of being a Peter Pan–absent dad while in actuality providing only a self-serving glamour of parenting.

This brings us to *Mrs. Doubtfire*, which marries these two archetypes. The absence here is the entire hook. Pantomime setup aside,[2] Doubtfire Dad wanted to be around his kids so badly he (a) committed some pretty serious crimes for a while, *against them*; (b) destroyed his identity and remade himself into a Jungian shadow figure riffing on Maria von Trapp and Mary Poppins;[3] and (c) thought this was a good idea.

There's a recut of the *Mrs. Doubtfire* trailer on YouTube where all they had to do was add some droning background music and put an eerie emphasis on the narrator's lines, and it legitimately feels like a horror movie premise. This flipa-roo works surprisingly well because *Mrs. Doubtfire's* premise

---

1. This isn't even necessarily articulated. "All that other stuff" doesn't even exist in this ultimate form of misogyny.

2. One critic slammed *Doubtfire* by saying the plot was just an excuse to let Williams go ham. I kind of dig that, but also have no problems with it? Like, let Williams go nuts. Please. We need more of that. Just extract it from the necessity of plot. That's the real problem here.

3. The best dads of all time?

is — once you remove Robin Williams's genius-level charisma and energy — a terrifying domestic situation.

Think about it. He's every woman's nightmare. A man you thought you knew, thought you could *trust*, tearing away any possibility of mutual understanding. Mrs. Doubtfire is a monster, in the truest sense of the word: something unknowable, and therefore rife with potential danger. In the movie we are saddled with sympathy for a monster,[1] because we see the world and the drama through his eyes, and because Robin Williams was a comedic genius.

There is no way that the reveal at the end would play out with the kids and mom being, like, "Oh, it was just Dad in a costume," as though he was Santa at a Christmas party, then let this serial-liar-and-fraudster creep back into their lives. The fact that this guy invaded your life post-court-order in disguise *and maintained that deception for months* is some trauma-worthy stuff. Seriously, if someone at Disney+ wanted to cash in on a gritty *Doubtfire* reboot, your framing narrative could be each of these kids going to therapy. There's plenty of material in there.

The true horror of *Mrs. Doubtfire* is exemplified by the fact that the dad had to destroy himself in order to portray a parent. He isn't becoming the real deal, don't let the ending fool you. He could have grown up thousands of times before his wife divorced him. No, he's not uniting the Jungian self with its shadow, but rather pouring it onto the mirror of his self and snorting the results. A man, the subtext tells us, could not do this. He needs to be a she to be free. Or at least *pretend* to be a she, putting on a latex-thin illusion predicated on stereotype and assumption.[2]

---

1. In a *way* more insidious way than Robin Williams's other everyday monster flick, *One Hour Photo*.

2. See *Tootsie* for a more direct example of this, where Dustin Hoffman's cross-dressing character can only learn to empathize and express feelings after donning the disguise of a woman.

Where *Hook* attempts to portray Robin Williams as a serious man struggling to rediscover his inner child, and *Aladdin's* Genie is an inner-child-enabler writ large with superhuman abilities, Mrs. Doubtfire is a mask that allows a man to make responsible parenting logistics "fun" by shedding the shackles of his gender and discovering the play in everyday life. Now that his character is allowed to express creativity within the domestic sphere, Williams doesn't have to rent a circus just to get his rocks off.

Throughout it all, the Robin Williams Dad is howling, howling against the emptiness within and the lack of connection without. He thinks, "If only I turn up the volume, maybe they'll hear me," and never, "I wonder what they're shouting, over there, as they run away from me."

·

The way these models of dadly absence shamble into real life are no less problematic. When you force a caring father to be absent, he tends to manifest that manic energy so well encapsulated in Robin Williams's comedy. It's building up all day, a heady cocktail of regret and hope, each moment of clarity subsumed with trying to think about ways to make up for lost time by cramming all of that missed opportunity into a condensed meaning-crystal through sheer will and bombast.

"Play! Play!" the absent dad screams (in his head) even as the child just wants to eat dinner or chill out after a long day doing just that. "More fun! More joy!"

This not only doesn't work, but it also makes you another monster. Instead of responding to the people around you and the actual social/emotional cues, this monster dad is demanding a fun-tribute that does not serve their kid. It serves the dad's needs, and uses the child as an emotional prop to hold up the dad's rickety sense of self-worth and uncertainty about the decisions they've made to build a life that does not fulfill anyone's deeper needs.

As we see in *Mrs. Doubtfire*, this energy also makes you a monster to the other adults in the room, who de facto become "the" adult in the room, since you can't even change your own emotional diaper.

Hell, kids don't even appreciate it. Since kids, especially young kids, live in a moment of eternal now (their minds mostly disconnected from causality and time) they don't feel nearly as much ongoing self-perpetuated pressure or intuitively understand how it could build up inside you all day long. Overcompensation weirds a kid out, because they just see you acting over the top and aren't comparing your behaviour to a logarithm of absence and longing. When a kid misses you, they miss you *right now*. When you're here, they're with you, 100 percent. They don't see (or hoard the regret of) missed opportunities. They only see the opportunity right in front of them that a "zany," overcompensating dad is burning by trying to force what ought to happen naturally.

A scheme of paternal overcompensation, like the one found in *Mrs. Doubtfire* or the newer, tragicomic version in *The Royal Tenenbaums*,[1] inevitably collapses under its own weight. The family is left with lies, and the father eventually — after all of his wild plans crash against the wall of reality — realizes he can't trick his way into people's hearts.

Thus the wacky dad is[2] forced to grow up. To build a real relationship, based on nothing more than authentically trying to *be there*. Doing the hard work they knew they should've

---

1. Where the mask is the father's illness, a ruse that grants him entry and sympathy after decades of abandonment.

2. Finally.

been doing all along, but thought they were too clever or eccentric for the rules to apply to them.

If it isn't too late, if they're lucky, they earn an epilogue.

Sadly, in real life, epilogues rarely occur.

Rambo's Big Tantrum

YOU KNOW, RAMBO IS A pretty weird story. Heck, it isn't even called "Rambo,"[1] it's called *First Blood*, which sounds like a mafia story, not a countercultural romp through the woods where a drifter (played by Sylvester Stallone) gets caught up in a one-man war against a local police force that spills out into the countryside, calls upon the National Guard, and, eventually, blows up a sleepy town alongside any lingering positive sentiments we might have entertained about how an empire like America treats the veteran survivors of its endless war machine.

That first Rambo story is so different from the gonzo cartoon pap that followed. *First Blood*, the book and the movie, is head and shoulders and rock-hard abs above every other iteration of Stallone's franchise-hungry sequels, because it has real emotional stakes. John Rambo is way more vulnerable, the story tracks a knife's plunge into the dark heart of masculinity, and the core conflict is a familial one. Rather than sic Rambo on another country like the subsequent movies, in this one he

---

1. Which is a kind of apple. One of the most iconic action movie characters of the '80s/all time is named after a goddamn apple cultivar.

is dealing with the relationship of the soldier to the fatherland, America, represented by two stand-in dad bods: the police and the army. The sheriff and the soldier. Dual representatives of America's iconic masculine authority figures, both amplified to thematic breaking point.

First Blood starts and ends with Rambo's two pseudo-dads. The first is Sheriff Teasle (played by Brian Dennehy), a small-town police officer who picks up a scruffy-haired vagrant on the highway and, rather than give him assistance, drives him to the far side of town and tells him to keep on walking. Turns out the vagrant is a Vietnam vet, a Green Beret named Rambo, and he's been pushed one too many times. Rambo disregards the sheriff's orders to move on, prompting his arrest.

Throughout this, and every other exchange Rambo and Teasle have, they exude a "punk son vs. hard-ass dad" energy. Rambo tries quiet rebellion, he tries emo looks, and he tries simple explanations of his needs. He just wanted a bite to eat. Teasle responds, again and again, with variations of "Respect my authority. Do as I say," in much the same way as a parent cajoling their recalcitrant toddler. "You can just impress the hell out of me," Teasle says as Rambo refuses to get fingerprinted, "by doing exactly as you're told." Teasle's tone, his exasperation at Rambo not doing what he's supposed to, his shortness with Rambo: I've been there a thousand times with my son, half an hour into trying to get him to put his pants on.

Down at the station, a couple of the sheriff's good ole boys have fun taunting, beating, and hosing Rambo down. Throughout, Rambo struggles against the officers, which only increases their belligerence, until one flashes a straight razor at him and Rambo freezes. He has a flashback to Nam. To being tortured by the Viet Cong. Then Rambo snaps. He beats the crap out of the entire police force and escapes into the woods on a stolen dirt bike.

The rest of the movie unfurls with that special action-movie causality where each set piece necessitates the next, with ever-increasing intensity. The police department stages a manhunt. Rambo turns it on them with handmade wooden traps. Instead of backing down, they call in the National Guard, they cordon off the countryside, and the whole fricassee becomes national news. This is when Rambo's second dad[1] shows up, Colonel Trautman (Richard Crenna), the avatar of the state. Through his tête-à-tête with Teasle, we learn about Rambo's super-soldier past.

Trautman trained Rambo into a killing machine who could fly a helicopter or drive a tank, fight with any weapon, or live off a diet of "things that would make a billy goat puke," while murdering as many enemy soldiers as possible. As a father figure, Trautman is distant, cold, and aloof. What's more, he only shows up halfway through the story, now that the conflict is national-news big, like the kind of dad who only cleans up his messes once someone finds out about them.

As Rambo's rampage intensifies, Trautman tries to manipulate him, calling on the names of their old (dead) war buddies, talking to Rambo about the good ole days when they slept in trees and drank napalm for breakfast. But it doesn't work. This kid has seen too much. He's been pushed too hard and too far by his terrible return to America, and he cannot stomach the institutional pep talk.

The cat-and-mouse game continues until Rambo commandeers a military truck, grabs a massive M60 machine gun, blows up a gas station, shoots out the town's power supply, destroys a few buildings, and barricades himself in the police station after shooting Teasle off the roof.

---

1. "I've come to get my boy," Trautman says in his intro scene. "I recruited him. I trained him. I commanded him in Vietnam for three years. I'd say that makes him mine."

The police and National Guard swarm around the police station. Before Rambo can finish Teasle off, Trautman stops him and gives Rambo one way out: surrender. When Rambo finally gives up, Stallone delivers a heart-rending speech that rushes out of him like a burst dam.

When Rambo came back to the States from Nam, he was spat on. Called a baby killer. Booted from one job to the next. Suffering silently from PTSD. He wandered the road, looking for the lost men from his fraternity of Green Berets. Seeking some semblance of that world of war, because it was based on honour. On a code. "You watch my back, I'll watch yours." It made sense. Here, in the heart of the empire, nothing makes sense and there's nobody to watch your back. Here, Rambo can't even buy a burger without getting kicked out of town by a small-town sheriff whose world view is less expansive than his belt.

All of those emotions. All of those shitty experiences. All of that pain and confusion. The poor guy just needed a friend. Rambo was bottling up all of that rage and all of that betrayal (a country he gave his life to, that he saw his friends give their lives to, absurd deaths that meant nothing strategically to the war effort, beautiful lives lost for nothing) that only break out of him when he is pushed to the absolute limits of human endurance *and* because his imperial dad is there, giving Rambo one last chance to end his war.

Then he is arrested. That's the movie's answer to the grim question, "What can we do with our veterans?" We transform these boys into killing machines, and when they spurt a little oil and show a few sparks after they survive the maw of destruction, well, I guess we ship them off to a little grey box somewhere so they don't bother the rest of these nice folks with their caterwauling.

That's the real ticket that empire punches for her soldiers. Come back home and you're on your own.

If Trautman is a cut-out of the system, the cold, uncaring infrastructure of empire and state, then Teasle stands in for the other side of the fatherland, the folk. Teasle is a symbol of the everyday alienation Rambo endured after coming home. The omnipresent need to conform, threatening ostracization for any breach of etiquette or decorum.

Neither has any real time for a troubled guy like Rambo. Neither is willing or able to give him what he needs: a hug. An ear to listen to. Hell, it takes destroying a town before anyone will even give Rambo the time of day, and when he finally breaks down it's with tears that he surrenders, clutching on to Trautman's uniform like a baby clinging to its mother.

.

Like any rip-roaring movie plot, it all feels rather deterministic, and yet the main players had an opportunity to avert disaster.

The choice appears in a keystone scene right after Rambo escapes from the police station. He vanishes into the mountainside forest like a ghost. When Teasle and the boys come after him, Rambo takes them out, one by one, using guerilla tactics but — and this is crucial — he refrains from killing them.[1] He then ambushes Teasle and holds him against a tree with that massive iconic Rambo bowie knife and says, "I could've killed them all. I could've killed you. In town you're the law, out here it's me. Don't push it. Don't push it. I'll give you a war you won't believe." Then he angles the knife against Teasle's jaw so that he's forced to make eye contact. Rambo growls, "Let it go. Let it go." He takes Teasle's rifle[2] and stalks off into the underbrush.

---

1. This was a conscious decision on Stallone's part, as he wanted Rambo to be a sympathetic character. In fact, he doesn't directly kill anyone.

2. And symbol of masculinity! To correct this spiritual castration, the first thing Teasle does when he goes back to the police station is unlock a big ole vault full of guns. Whew! Manliness restored.

All Teasle has to do is reject a core tenet of insecure masculinity. All he has to do is be the bigger man, and back down. Of course, he doesn't. He stubbornly refuses throughout the entire movie to bend in any way, shape, or form. Instead Teasle consistently ratchets up the stakes like a stubborn gambler throwing their house deed into the pot after losing their life savings.

This inability to be flexible, to adapt and respond with anything other than a greater intensity of aggression, trying to bark louder, shove harder, and out-stubborn the opposition is a useless methodology interwoven into the fragility of performing the male identity. It's in all the unwritten rules. A "real" man can never admit fault. Never back down. Never compromise. That's losing power, right, and patriarchy dictates that every social exchange is either a measure or exchange of power.

When you lay it all out, it sounds bananas, but I can readily admit that I absorbed and replicated that mode of behaviour. When emotions run high, the instinct to bury my heels and stand my ground is powerful, even to this day. If I'm wrong, my knee-jerk reaction is to double down and concoct an elaborate scaffolding to justify my position. I have to fight this tendency, which is only possible when I'm aware of how much of a buffoon I'm being.

Thankfully, my toddler has shown me just how incredibly ineffective this approach really is. You see, every clash with a toddler is like *First Blood*. If you meet them head-on, demand for demand, volume against volume, you will lose every single time. In the exact same way that Teasle's call on a manhunt, a helicopter, or the National Guard leads to Rambo coming at him even harder — a toddler will consistently outmanoeuvre, outgun, and out-stubborn any direct confrontation, no matter how you escalate it.[1]

---

1. Within reason, of course.

A toddler is just as much a force of nature as Rambo. Both have nothing to lose. They are totally okay with amplifying a conflict so that it takes over their entire life, whereas we have things we need to do. Errands, a job, or even etiquette to maintain. A toddler doesn't care. They will thrash on the ground while screaming bloody murder if you suggest that they have to wear their red boots instead of their blue shoes because it is raining outside. They want the blue shoes. That is all they know. That is their entire world, and they will fight tooth and nail to get what they want. Just like Rambo, they've been pushed too far, one too many times, and they will give you a war you won't believe.

This is why some of the best parenting advice for toddlers is to creatively incorporate their needs when they're acting truculent. Connect with what they're saying first, then (and only then) redirect that conflict-energy toward the productive thing that you need to do. Connect and redirect. Bend and flow. Give them a few wins throughout the day, so that they feel heard and respected, and they'll be far more pliable. It's a dance, a give and a take, and it nips so many tantrums right in the bud.

Halfway through the movie, when things are pretty obviously going poorly for the sheriff's department, Trautman suggests similar tactics for dealing with Rambo. Trautman understands how to manipulate his boy's emotional needs. He explains to Teasle, "Let him go. For now. Diffuse the whole situation. Diffuse him. Provide a little gap and let him slip through it. Then put out a nationwide APB. In a couple of weeks, you'll pick him up in Seattle or someplace, working in a car wash. There'll be no fight and nobody else will get hurt." That's a creative bit of distraction! Letting Rambo feel like he's the one making the choice is a top-notch toddler parenting tip.

However, Teasle's ego can't even process the suggestion. He's locked in: to doing things his way, to being in charge, to asserting his authority, and having everyone follow his plan. Teasle is both the bad-news authoritarian dad and the sleep-deprived pushed-to-their-limits parent who just wants this fight to end. Now. Teasle's trapped in that terrible feedback loop of trying bad, short-term solutions because the long-term problem-solving feels like giving in. It feels like giving up power. Like it diminishes him in some way, because his identity is predicated on building and maintaining power over others at all cost.

That's no way to parent, and no way to problem solve.

None of it works with Rambo. None of it works with kids. Don't push it. Pushing only results in pushback.

Take Rambo's advice: Let it go. Think like Trautman: Circumnavigate the immediate issue. Get creative. Otherwise, like Teasle, you're just as responsible for the tantrum. More so, I'd wager, since you ought to know better. A toddler can't, that's not their job.

It's ours.

The Sitcom Dad

NOWADAYS, WHEN ONE PONDERS SITCOM DADS, the two words that come to mind are "bumbling" and "inept." Sure, we might like the guy, but core to his character is a chronic incompetence. In his job, his adult relationships, and, worst of all, as a dad. Homer Simpson is the obvious example, a character so lazy and unfit for parenting that in an episode where he is expressly trying to up his dad game,[1] his son, Bart, says, "Your half-assed under-parenting was a lot more fun than your half-assed over-parenting."

Don't get me wrong, I loved *The Simpsons* like only a child of the '90s could. My fledgling brain was forged by this show. I haven't seen an episode in at least fifteen years, but I could quote back to you any number of scenes from that golden era from season 3 to somewhere between seasons 7 and 9.[2] Heck, one of the most successful essays I ever wrote was about the need for *The Simpsons* to die, as a work, so that we could place

---

1. Season 6, episode 10, "Grampa vs. Sexual Inadequacy."

2. I'm sure some other scholars have pieced together the descent of the show, but for me, the tragic death of Phil Hartman spelled the end of *The Simpsons*.

it within its proper historical context, rather than watch it wither on in zombie format, losing relevance with each shambling year as the undead lose limbs.[1]

I loved *The Simpsons*, and yet I can say with perfect honesty that Homer is a distillate of all of the worst traits a father could possibly possess.

Homer is a narcissist, a glutton, a sloth, a boor, a bore, a moron, and a petty tyrant. He's violent, sexist, doesn't listen, has no work ethic, undermines his wife, bullies his children, spends all his free time at a dank sewer of a bar or watching television, and is an indifferent father at the best of times who perpetuates the myth that men are like bears — the best we can hope from them is that they'll ignore their children.

He's just so infuriating, when seen through the lens of a dad bod. A shocking disavowal of the role and its importance or value. A perfect *Akira*-like monstrosity of tendrils and limbs conglomerated from all of television's history through the brain trust of early *Simpsons* writers and their encyclopedic knowledge of twentieth-century American history, spurted back out in a form that would, much to their simultaneous chagrin and joy, metastasize beyond its initial frame at an unbelievable rate.

•

It's honestly kind of a shock that people kept making regular sitcoms after *The Simpsons* reached its cultural zenith. That's one of those weird aspects of culture and the plodding waltz of history,[2] compared to, say, science, one of the

1. I received an email from the office of the CEO of Fox the day that essay was published. They said that they "liked my ideas," which was the last thing I'd expect to hear from a television studio. I was couch surfing at a friend's house in Oxford, England, at the time. It was a very surreal moment.

2. One step forward, three steps left, two steps backward, three steps right.

more successful endeavours of iterative human intervention. Once someone figures something out in the hard sciences, like, say, that mice don't spontaneously generate if you leave a rag and some cheese in the closet,[1] after it becomes generally accepted,[2] you don't get a crew of neo-revisionist scientists charging in a few years later, stuffing closets with different kinds of cheese *just in case*.

In television, it isn't just Homer who's lazy. The general culture machine is made up of cranks who just want to turn the wheel and spurt out the lowest common denominator. So even though we already have the pinnacle of terribad sitcom father, and even though that show is *still airing* and is a monolith of popular culture, someone thought it was a good idea to keep spinning out photocopies of the same character with different BMIs, haircuts, and jobs, and who live in different parts of the country.

Culture operates on a different metaphor than science. Culture operates like a virus, mutating as many variations as possible in order to infect as many subjects as possible. No wonder we now have a million variations of Homer Simpson, each splinter taking one of those brilliantly condensed satirical features of the bumbling sitcom father and splicing out mutation after mutation. Each one diluting the collective unconscious idea of dadhood. Each one eroding our sense that a dad can

---

1. This used to be a thing! People believed in spontaneous generation. Another recipe for creating life *ex nihilo*: leave a bit of meat out for a few weeks and it will grow maggots! Brilliant!

2. Okay, I admit, there could be some better processes in place here. The history of science has all kinds of squabbles before the dust settled, and when regular people see these nuanced, caveat-riddled arguments between experts they think, "Ah, those nerds don't know nuthin'," despite the fact that, in general, while scientists may disagree about the amplitude of conclusions, they usually have a pretty good co-operative understanding of the premises. The problem is that everyone thinks in terms of eggs/cholesterol in the '80s, which is more the fault of science journalism than science itself.

be something other than a bumbler, or in some essential way a failure, as this mythopoetic image writes the fundamental creative imaginary each and every time it is propagated.

•

Homer may be the nadir of a bad dad bod, but he is joined by a generation of televised fathers who serve a fairly singular narrative purpose: to be the butt of the joke. Tim the Toolman Taylor in *Home Improvement*, Al Bundy in *Married … with Children*, Ray Barone in *Everybody Loves Raymond*, and Phil Dunphy in *Modern Family* all oscillate between different shades of incompetence: man-child, lazy slob, clueless goof, and oblivious narcissist. Their antics may prime the pump for situational comedy to occur, but the cost is perpetuating the stereotype that competent nurturing and caring is somehow unnatural for menfolk.

What's more, these Sitcom Dads and their ilk all lean so hard on their wives to maintain the necessary rhythms of life. These men do their jobs, often begrudgingly, then they come home and they *tap out*. The worst of these characters are glued to their couches, and we watch them watching television in a voyeuristic mirror of metafiction. Meanwhile, their wives (who are also working) take care of the domestic chores and emotional labour so that the house doesn't fall down around their ears and the children don't descend into a feral, *Lord of the Flies*–esque state.

Sitcoms are honestly a nightmare vision of the modern family. Remove the laugh track from these shows and the howl of the void echoes between the canyons of fatherly ineptitude.

What's totally wild is that these modern dad bods are a cheap facsimile of the father figures who graced the silver screen of yore.

•

When your traditional Sitcom Dad comes home, the rest of his family is already there: watching television, cooking dinner, playing in the backyard. He takes off his coat, or his hat. Depending on the era and social class he drops a briefcase or a steel lunch box, takes off his shoes, and dumps his car keys somewhere near the door.

Daddy's home. He says the catchphrase. The laugh track cheers in canned enthusiasm.

A stand-in for the status quo, for the wider world (from whence he came at the beginning of the episode: that place filled with other adult men who are doing real work and making the world, not like this domestic space of sound and fury that signifies nothing), the traditional Sitcom Dad is a quick barometer check for the audience — to telegraph that, yes, this is a funny story. What's more, the traditional Sitcom Dad acts as a microcosm for the great myth of non-serialized television: nothing ever truly changes.

No matter what antics the kids get up to, the Sitcom Dad has the answer. He smooths over problems with a gentle but firm hand, his behaviour modelling a better way.

Think of Ward Cleaver from *Leave It to Beaver*, Mike Brady from *The Brady Bunch*, or the ultimate old-school dad bod, Andy Taylor on *The Andy Griffith Show*. Good, competent dads patiently enduring hijinks and dispensing tidbits of homespun wisdom to end each episode.

Within these fictional worlds, Dad's authority is sacrosanct, his position cosmic. He is the family's conduit to the greater hierarchy, and, therefore, father knows best.

Sure, maybe he's a bit detached, a bit lacking in the emotional expression department, and a puritanical stickler for the obvious basics of good midcentury American morals: thrift, hygiene, and manners. And I'm 100 percent happy to admit that the gender dynamics are completely bananas in these shows. I'm not saying these are perfect dad bods, by any stretch of the imagination, but at least the traditional Sitcom Dad is modelling fatherhood. At least they are parents, instead of one more kid their wife has to take care of.

·

Big claims call for big evidence. Thankfully, academics have studied the descent of Sitcom Dad bods in the latter half of the twentieth century. Not only did they find that there was a stark shift from the depiction of wise competence (in the sitcoms of the 1950s and 1960s) to foolish goofballs and bumbling oafs (in the 1970s and 1980s),[1] but they also tracked the ever-increasing likelihood that the father would be the butt of the joke.[2] Initially, this shift of the butt of the joke from the mother to the father was interpreted as an incorporation of feminist values, as the father transitioned from paragon to "fair game," and the increasing depiction of women as competent breadwinners led to stronger, supra-capable mother characters.

However, this trend, like all Hollywood meme production, kept on growing until we found ourselves in the straits we're in today: the dads can barely tie their shoes and the moms are doing everything. Recent studies reflect that, too. In a stupendously thorough "quantitative content analysis" study published in 2021, Scharrer et al.[3] investigated 578 scenes from

1. Murial G. Cantor, "Prime-time Fathers: A Study in Continuity and Change," *Critical Studies in Mass Communications* 7, no. 3 (1990): 275–85, tandfonline.com /doi/abs/10.1080/15295039009360179.

2. Erica Sharrer, "From Wise to Foolish: The Portrayal of the Sitcom Father, 1950s–1990s," *Journal of Broadcasting and Electronic Media* 45, no. 1 (2001): 23–40, tandfonline.com/doi/abs/10.1207/s15506878jobem4501_3.

3. E. Scharrer et al., "Disparaged Dads? A Content Analysis of Depictions of Fathers in U.S. Sitcoms Over Time," *Psychology of Popular Media* 10, no. 2 (2021): 275–87, doi.apa.org/doiLanding?doi=10.1037%2Fppm0000289.

thirty-four top-rated, family-centred sitcoms from 1980 to 2017 to specifically explore the depiction of fatherhood. They isolated two aspects of that depiction: (a) whether the father is participating in "disparagement humour," in other words is he being made fun of or is he making fun of someone else, and (b) how often dads are portrayed with their kids doing three key parenting interactions: giving advice, setting rules, or positively or negatively reinforcing their kids' behaviour.

After crunching all that raw data, they found that modern TV dads are simply not depicted doing parenting. Recent sitcoms portray dads doing the three interactions listed above in fewer scenes than older shows. What's more, when they do parent, there is a distinct correlation between a growth in disparagement humour aimed at dads: 18 percent of scenes from the 1980s prompted audiences to laugh at a father's parental incompetence, poor judgment, or childish behaviour; 31 percent of scenes in the 1990s had this "humorously foolish" fathering; and just over 50 percent of the relevant scenes in sitcoms from the 2000s and 2010s pointed a big ole Nelson Muntz finger at dad's attempt to be a father, and laughed. *Ha-haw!*

That's one hockey stick of a graph!

I blame Homer. On the one hand, his creators took the worst traits of fathers and mashed them all together into a single bald yellow monstrosity. On the other, *The Simpsons* has been around for too long, been too popular and critically acclaimed for Homer's formula to *not* get ripped off a thousand times, and thus poison the concept of sitcom fatherhood.

I hear the counter-argument coming in from the back: "But Homer's *funny*! These qualities are what make for the funniest Sitcom Dad, and that's the whole point."

Is it? Are they? Is this descent a necessary condition resulting from the needs of sitcom narrative structure, the comedic reproducibility of Homer Simpson's character traits, and the momentum from television production's maximal output churn?

.

If we did a kind of icon-ectomy, a bit of conceptual surgery, and took away all of the shitty parts of Homer Simpson, could we not still have a funny Sitcom Dad? Like Jack Nicholson in the diner scene from *Five Easy Pieces*, desperate for a piece of toast, I'm saying hold the self-obsession, hold the incompetence, hold the terrible lack of communication and the resentful co-dependent partnership, but bring me a thick slice of bumbling and some fresh-squeezed lack of awareness. Not only would that still be funny, and perform the structural/narrative role of the Sitcom Dad, but that kind of a dad could be fuelled by something other than ineptness. He could be misguided, out of his element, or competent but missing the mark. Better yet, he could be fuelled by love and connection, rather than resentment and nihilism. I'd argue that dad bod already exists, stretched out and smiling awkwardly on the other side of the Sitcom Dad couch, in the guise of Johnny Rose from *Schitt's Creek*.

Schitt's Creek is a sitcom produced by the CBC that aired from 2015 to 2020, and its final season swept all seven major comedy awards at the seventy-second Primetime Emmy Awards. The show follows the formerly wealthy Rose family, who lose their fortune and are forced to live in a motel together in a small rural town that they once bought as a joke. Throughout the series, the family adjusts to a life without wealth and the fact that they now live together in tight quarters, constantly getting in each other's business.

Johnny Rose (played by Canadian comedy legend Eugene Levy) used to be the CEO of a video store franchise. Moira

Rose (Canadian comedy legend Catherine O'Hara[1]), his wife, was a soap-opera star. Their adult children, David (Dan Levy) and Alexis (Annie Murphy), were a dilettante art world fashionista and party girl gallivanter, respectively. They are all fish out of water in Schitt's Creek, a cute anytown, and the show tracks their trials and tribulations as they acclimatize, adjust their priorities, set new goals, and — dare I say it — grow as people.

In the middle of it all, trying to be a rock for his family, Johnny Rose is as real a dad as they come. Sure Johnny's goofy, and ofttimes oblivious, but the core of this man is care for his family, and he possesses a surprising competence beneath his shaken sense of self-esteem.

For every wretched quality of Homer Simpson, Johnny plays a ribald counterpoint, and maybe it's just because it's Eugene Levy (and he has those damn eyebrows) but he is easily as funny as the other characters in this hilarious show.

Let's do a classic character sketch:

Johnny Rose loves his family. He is devoted to them. He may not know how to express that emotion all the time, and he may be overbearing in how he does choose to show his affection — but those foibles serve the dual purpose of letting the family know that he loves them *and* making him a funnier character. See, we're already off to a good start with plain old emotional expression.

Johnny is also an incredible partner. He supports Moira. He knows how to put himself and his needs second to hers in pretty much every other episode. When she wants to run for town council, he quietly puts away his own desire to do so. They are infatuated with each other, aren't afraid to let

---

1. You know, the mom from *Home Alone*. Also won an Emmy for her writing in *Second City Television*. Starred in Christopher Guest's mockumentaries like *Waiting for Guffman*, *Best in Show*, and *A Mighty Wind*.

each other know it, and they play an equal role in supporting each other's weaknesses and bolstering each other's emotional well-being.

Even at the beginning of the show, when the family is still trying to figure out how to be a family unit after years of living separate lives, these two core competencies of Johnny's stand out and mark him as taking on that traditional Sitcom Dad role of the central pillar tying everyone together. The difference here is that, unlike on the vast majority of sitcoms,[1] the family learns to live *together*: they all learn how to communicate, put themselves second, and think not only of each other, but of "others" at all.

I'm not saying that Johnny spurs that growth on — he is but one participant in that quadrangle of development — but he pulls the initial weight and attempts (often awkwardly, with those eyebrows) to express to everyone the opportunity for growth that they've been forced into through the life-shattering loss of fortunes that sees them shacking up together in a roadside motel.

To continue with the bullet list, unlike many modern Sitcom Dads, Johnny has ambition. Rather than be a personification of resentful inertia, Johnny's got hustle. He is not content to take the licking fate has bestowed upon his family, and he works — incrementally, iteratively, step by painful step — toward his goals. He models active problem-solving and goal setting, as well as trying to talk about motivation when his family encounters issues of their own. He's off-base (and hilarious) when trying to tackle these subjects head-on, but as a model of behaviour he's pretty darn inspiring! What's more, he learns from his experiences, adapts his mindset, and *tries again*. Meaning he's also a subtle, realistic model of resilience.

---

1. And, sadly, most of television.

Taking that trait a step further, Johnny also actively supports his family's dreams, whereas Homer is pathologically incapable of maintaining a picture of another human being in his head, let alone understanding what their ambitions might be. Whether it's supporting his son's same-sex relationship or business, his daughter's return to college and entrepreneurship, his wife's ridiculous acting career — Johnny sees how these aspirations matter to his family, and he is behind them with everything he's got.

This ties back all the way to the core principle of being a dad: you aren't the main character anymore, and that has a really nifty metafictional layer to it.

Schitt's Creek is actually Dan Levy's project. Dan Levy is Eugene Levy's real-life son. I can only imagine that having your dad, *EUGENE LEVY*, pulling for you helps get a project off the ground, maybe get a good word in with Catherine O'Hara, tilt the ear of executives at CBC. In other words, as rad a dad as Johnny Rose is, it would seem that the character doesn't fall too far from the actor tree. He agreed to star in a pitch-perfect swan-song role, and has taken a back seat in terms of allowing his son to get the credit where it's due for creating this incredible piece of twenty-first-century television.

Johnny's awkwardness, his, let's be frank, cringier dadliness,[1] his attempts at caring that come off as "too much," or how he gets in his own way by being such an awesome try-hard — in other words, the bumbles — mix so perfectly with the sweet bits that they are simultaneously made *more funny* and make us root for the Rose family so much more than we would otherwise, if the care and attention to crafting a sympathetic, loving father figure wasn't present in the fiction.

---

1. Like the fact that he's an absolutely terrible gift-giver, whose gifts often insult the recipient.

And he's funny. Each of these elements plays naturally into the central character trait of the modern Sitcom Dad: Johnny tries his best, he isn't totally self-aware, he overplays his hand, and suffers from a bit of old-fashioned hubris — and these characteristics twine with his sweet spots to make for a character who has true dimension. His good spots make him sympathetic, help us root for him, and graft our happiness to his throughout his journey into more and more devoted fatherhood. As his family succeeds in growing into the people they were always meant to become, we can share with Johnny's pride and happiness alongside them. He's a portal to caring more deeply about the other characters in this wonderful slice of entertainment.[1]

•

Which takes us back to unfortunate Homer. Like I said, I loved that show as a teenager, but it reeks of '90s nihilism.[2] There is no redeeming Homer. No sympathy. No reason to root for him. Even in an episode that is ostensibly about developing self-awareness through a mystical spirit journey,[3] any pathos is reduced to cliché or parody for a quick gag. The show *sometimes* gives some sympathetic stories to Lisa or Bart, like in the episode with Dustin Hoffman as a substitute teacher who inspires Lisa to be her own person,[4] or when Bart, you know, literally sells his soul to Milhouse and must earn it back through existential suffering,[5] but Homer is left out in the cold.

---

1. Seriously. I watched this show throughout the pandemic. Its ray of real-ass sunshine is exactly what the doctor ordered for 2020–22.

2. To be fair, so did I back then.

3. Season 8, episode 9, "El Viaje Misterioso De Nuestro Jomer."

4. Season 2, episode 19, "Lisa's Substitute."

5. Season 7, episode 4, "Bart Sells His Soul."

I'd say rightly so, except that it exacerbates the point: a dad so consistently portrayed as such a narcissistic imbecile allows dud dads the world over to get away with acting like that. The model propagates, along the channel of the meme or the virus, and, as pathetic as it is, people repeat what they see.

In that way, we are barely different from kids.

Contra to Johnny, dad bods poured from Homer Simpson's mould don't have a sympathetic leg to stand on. No goals. No growth. No portal to caring for others. No justification for his foibles, no larger picture for ... anything. Both types are affably oblivious, but Johnny proves that Sitcom Dads can do *so much more* than merely turn the joke-crank and hope that laughs come out.

Part of the reason those studies that show how Sitcom Dads went from wise patriarch to nutty buffoon gall me so much is that trajectory contradicts my lived experience. The dads I know in real life are all trying their absolute damnedest to be a better person, a better kind of man, a better partner, and a better dad. The artistic laziness at the core of the bumbling dad trope yanks my chain, so to speak, in myriad dimensions.

Calling on social science again, in 2019 the Pew Research Center released some hot facts tracking American perceptions of fatherhood.[1] The key takeaways: Dads are spending triple the amount of time on child care as they did in 1965, they are just as likely as mothers to say that being a parent is "extremely important to their identity," and they find parenting a rewarding experience.

Real dads these days are *in it*, more than ever before. It's only fitting that a hybrid example as rich as Johnny Rose has been received with such widespread fanfare. We needed it. Part

---

1. Gretchen Livingston and Kim Parker, "8 Facts about American Dads," Pew Research Centre, June 12, 2019, pewresearch.org/fact-tank/2019/06/12/fathers-day-facts/.

bumbler, to ease our understanding of his role and disposition; part competent father figure, to show us how much more work there is to do — Johnny is a bridge between the Sitcom Dad bods of yesteryear, the bumbling nitwits of the twentieth century, and the unarticulated possibility space of dads to come.

The whimsical social realism of Dan Levy's utterly refreshing sitcom provides a depiction of fatherhood that resonates with the absolute pith of healthy, growing dad bods.

Try, and fail. Try again, try harder. Fail differently. Learn. Adapt.

Be there. Show up. Every single day.

Bumble toward the dad bod you want to be.

The Distant Driven Dad

HE'S PROBABLY A DOCTOR OR a scientist or an engineer. Occupations connected to a cold, objectifying force. A discipline that reduces events and people to hard numbers. A project that is so rarefied and removed from day-to-day life that it is eminently justifiable for it to be more important than a partner or a child. They can argue it, and they will, with a meticulous array of facts in a clear chain of inference and logic. Heck, these dads are also likely to argue the incredibly blinkered point that the work they're doing, that they've devoted their life to, that drives them so hard and so far away (from you) is more important than they are. It's bigger than them, so of course it's bigger than you. Never mind the fact that if it was so much bigger than them, then they could step away from the field and it would be just fine[1] and carry on without them. Oh no, don't suggest that, you wouldn't want to pierce their gargantuan egos.

The Distant Driven Dad bod is a *deus otiosus*. A dad who thinks of himself as a god among men, connected at the hip to

---

1. Which is, in many ways, the basis of contemporary science — there are fewer and fewer lone Newton-like geniuses anymore.

some noble quest that takes him away from the banal tasks of life, like caring for other people or being a part of their lives or cleaning up the messes they invariably leave behind them.

Oh yeah, their kids are one of those messes.

•

Generally, the kids are the protagonists, and these dads hover somewhere in the plot as either supporting characters or elusive and mysterious thematic figureheads.

A great and well-known example is Dr. Henry Jones Sr. in *Indiana Jones and the Last Crusade*, the third movie in the iconic pulp archaeology series. Played by Sean Connery, he ticks every box: he wasn't around when Indiana Jones was a kid, because he was off chasing the Holy Grail[1] through the study of medieval literature. This was a resentment-sponge for Indy, as well as a spur. Indiana wanted to get his dad's wayward attention, so the poor kid got into archaeology — even harder-core history than medieval literature, *Dad*. Not only that, he became the best gosh darn archaeologist he could, based on tenure, class size, ability to punch Nazis, and the probable contribution his artifact haul added to the historical record. All so that his dad might recognize him, give him a little tousle on the head, and say, "Attaboy."

Dr. Jones Sr. does none of the above; instead he vanishes off the face of the earth. This means that Indiana's relationship to his father is frozen at that moment of emotional separation: Indy still relates to his father as an adolescent. Even though they reconcile throughout (on the crucible of faith and the wonders of globe-trotting adventure), they don't really transcend the petulant framing of the way their codes of masculinity tie them together.

---

1. Like, the actual cup.

In fact, I'd reckon that this inability for the father and the son to grow into adult roles has stymied Indiana's personal self-image. He is basically a teenager stuck inside Harrison Ford's square and bristly jaw. Running on instinct, with zero ability to calculate danger, terrible communication with romantic partners, and a robust rebellious streak against authority, makes for a great action hero with lots of spicy moments — and, let's be frank, it's Han all over again — but a self-assured and self-actualized adult, Indy is not. He's got a chip on his shoulder. He's got something to prove, and this daddy complex of his is undoubtedly at the root of it.

Even though that terrible *Indiana Jones* reboot from 2008 is all about placing Harrison in the role of a father figure to Shia LaBeouf,[1] it is actually kind of impossible to imagine Indiana Jones as a dad. My mind hits a smooth, frictionless crystal wall when I try to picture what the heck that dynamic would be like, because Indiana is predicated on a kind of cartoon-person who, like Scrooge McDuck or Bugs Bunny, cannot actually have children.

It is not impossible to imagine Sean Connery's Jones Sr. chilling with a pipe, taking little Indy[2] and his dog to play some soccer, then reading a stack of xeroxed history papers and completely missing his son's game-winning header. Then, during the drive home, Connery would crack wise about why didn't Indy play a more sensible sport, like cricket.

Indiana can't grow up because he is trying to replicate and one-up his father, rather than become his own person and exist with his father as an equal. The relationship that Dr. Jones Jr. and Sr. have is like Zeno's Paradox; for every step that Indy takes along the same path, his dad has already taken two. Any

---

1. The Beef!
2. Yes, I know his name is Henry, but that's too jarring.

time Indy closes the distance, it is only by half. He cannot win a race against this father's experience.

Surprisingly, his father can't grow up either. Dr. Jones Sr. is just as trapped in this dynamic as Indy, with a perpetual need to one-up his son and parade that he was all up in there before Indiana was. Whether it's a sexual (what's a better word than "conquest"?) adventure, or an idea to escape from a trap, Connery's constant need to compete with his son is fine for a ribald-buddy action movie, but sad and pathetic when you see dads dunk on their kids in real life.

Until the climax, when they unite in purpose on Henry Sr.'s near-death. Only when they cease to race and instead stand shoulder to shoulder, Indiana building off his father's lifelong body of research, can they get anything done and begin the process of transcending their toxic cohabited adolescence.

Plus I guess they were made immortal? That's a pretty great ending.

•

The dynamic at play with this dad bod is how distance compels. How the absence of the father's heart (whether physical or emotional) can warp and bend the growth of any child. Toward or away, the forces of the Distant Driven Dad are always extreme.

Here's another example: *Locke*, an absolutely bananas movie starring Tom Hardy. The pitch is nuts: the entire movie is Tom Hardy's character, Ivan Locke, driving down the highway, talking to people on the phone. That's it. That's all you see. It's Tom Hardy's face for eighty-five *absolutely riveting* minutes on the M6 motorway between Birmingham and London.

Here's the deal: Ivan Locke is a construction foreman. Locke is *the man* when it comes to concrete. Scoff if you will, but big pours of concrete are insane engineering and logistical feats. The single night that the film portrays is a big one for concrete: Ivan Locke was supervising the largest non-nuclear, non-military pour[1] in European history — until he got a call from Bethan that she was going into labour. The twist is, Bethan is not his partner. Bethan is a colleague with whom Locke had a one-night stand seven months ago. It was the only time he ever cheated on his wife, and now the stork's come home with the bill.

Throughout the film, Locke drives down the highway and talks to several people: his boss, his colleague, his wife, his kids, nurses at the hospital, a politician, Bethan, and even an imaginary version of his own absentee father — and we see the active dismantling of a man, his work, his dreams, his family, all from a single mistake made late one night on the outskirts of Croydon.

Why on earth would this guy throw everything away?

So that he wouldn't make the same mistake his father did. Ivan Locke's father abandoned his family when Locke was a kid. Ivan never forgave his father, and vowed never to repeat the same mistake. Locke is categorically driven to be present in his child's life, even though he has no romantic feelings for Bethan, and even though it will destroy the life that he has built for himself, block by block, with an engineer's rigorous attention to detail.

Central to Locke's personality is this kind of clockwork precision for every single detail. First, we see it with the pour[2] as he lays out, step by step, the meticulous arrangements for this 200+ cement truck job, to his hapless second-in-command. This poor bloke is freaking out, he can't handle it all, but Locke

---

1. That's what they call it, "The Pour," as though it is a proper noun. The act of pouring concrete a kind of living being like some elemental. The spirit of the concrete.

2. "The Pour." Imagine it in a crisp, almost tweedy British accent but coming out of Tom Hardy.

is like, "Look, it's all in the binder. I will walk you through it. Concrete is an art. Concrete is a process. I will guide the concrete from here, with my words, like a wizard of liquid stone." He knows every single step of how to get that wet rock to form the perfect slab.

Then you see the same attention to detail in every other aspect of his life: his understanding that tonight is a bad night to miss because his boys are excited about the big football game that they were going to share together; heck, even the way he outlines his infidelity to his wife is kind of cruel because he doesn't spare any details for how meaningless the entire experience was for him. Just a moment of weakness. He has obviously been thinking about it *a lot* in the past seven months, and trying to figure out his plan of attack, before this baby decided to pop out a few months early, messing up his *plans*, man.

Lastly, you see it in how he lays out the moral argument for doing what he's doing. He doesn't care — or, no, he cares *immensely* — about each of the things that this decision is destroying, but he has done the math, so to speak, and come out on the side of being there when the baby is born, come hell or high water, and doing what he can to be there for this child of his.

When I say "categorically driven," I mean it. This guy is *Kantian* in the way he rips down the highway on a crash course with the singular moral modality that this decision wreaks upon the rest of his life. He is compelled to do this because *it is the right thing to do*, which also makes it the only thing that he can do. He doesn't feel like he has a choice, which does not free him from the burden, far from it, but instead figuratively plants his feet in concrete blocks as he leaps off London Bridge.

Again, why is he doing this? Because he has to one-up *his* dad, who wasn't there for him. The anti–Dr. Jones, Locke seeks to undo the damage that was done to him by breaking the cycle with his bastard child. It's a wild bit of nobility. The artistic decision to film the entire movie in a car rolling down the actual highway, with no other actors present onscreen as Locke makes thirty-six phone calls on his way to the hospital, transforms this movie into a freakishly powerful meditation on that single decision and its cascade of consequences.

Yet Locke is in the selfsame Zeno's Paradox as Indiana Jones. He can never defeat his father, made clear in all of these weird "conversations" that Locke has with his father's phantasm. Locke will be carrying that ghost till the day he dies, and the most he can do is not spawn another in Bethan's child.

For all his presumed moral simplicity, Locke is a complicated dad bod, wedged between distance and intimacy. On the side of distance, the fact that he could keep all of this from his wife, from his kids, during all this time as he concocted a plan as intricate as the big pour means that he's a skillful dissembler. On the other hand, there is a real emotional current running between Locke and his family. So the guy has done the work of being a good dad.

Still, I can't ignore the fact that he is literally distant from everyone and everything that matters to him throughout the entirety of this film, locked as he is in this car barrelling down the highway. The decisions he makes to prop up this sole moral stand push him further and further away from his family. It's almost too on the nose to point out how driven this guy is. He's literally driving a car, he's behind the wheel, he has the choice to turn around at any time, and yet he maintains his heading and his velocity, running forward, toward this abstraction that is causing very real pain and suffering in the people that supposedly matter the most in the world to him.

Well, it seems like they don't matter quite so much as how high you can hoist your petard, Ivan.

Again, in attempting to erase the impact of his own Distant Driven Dad bod, Locke has merely shifted the detachment into another dimension. One where he can lie to his wife and children, buttressed by this notion that what he's doing is beyond that frame of morality. That he is serving a higher need, and not only does that need compel, it justifies.

.

The Distant Driven Dad bod blasts down the highway of life, leaving some child in its wake, a man so hell-bent on his own fortunes/ambition/vision that he can't see all the people coughing and choking on the exhaust behind him.

Dr. Jones is a solid intro, but he's still fun and plucky enough that we like him — what's more, he manages to begin the process of reconciliation with Indy through their shared hatred of fascism and delight in puzzle-solving their way to the Holy Grail. The fact that he convinces Indy to leave the cup as the dungeon falls apart, to give up the quest and the obsession, shows that he grew beyond this dad bod and, ultimately, cared more for his son than his drive.

Ivan Locke pours a thick slab over his entire existence, burying his job, his colleagues, and his family beneath the suffocation of his own guilt and hardline engineer's ethic. He cleaves to his moral line severely, unable to compromise with himself, and therefore unwilling to compromise with anyone else. His world is black and white — or, rather, his world is the moral grey of wet cement, and Locke believes that the only way to influence that grey world is by strict adherence to a rigid set of standards. By acting as though the world can be controlled by treating it in binaries. As though through sheer dint of will and sticking to his moral guns, Locke believes he can be the frame and lathe that shapes the concrete into a perfectly flat, level surface. He believes he can control the raw material of life, which includes other people, if only he does so with enough preparation and consideration.

Locke's a great example of the Distant Driven Dad, except

DAD BOD   85

Locke's a great example of the Distant Driven Dad, except for one thing: his vision is pretty narrow. Just like the artistic decision to confine the film to one drive in one car down one highway with one actor, Locke's conflict and fortune/ambition/vision are exceedingly personal. This is one man's moral quandary, and he does a great job of inflating it to mammoth proportions, but I wouldn't say he quite fits the bill for the dad bod when it comes to conflating it to a universal dictum. Locke acts as though his drive is categorical, but it isn't the same as the scientist who abandons his son because he's looking for a cure for cancer. In other words, Locke acts the perfect Distant Driven Dad bod, despite missing a key ingredient in this cold curry.

•

For the truest embodiment of the Distant Driven Dad, we need to find a man whose ego and the scope of his ambition so thoroughly shatter the grade curve that there is no way to express it using realistic terms. Something epic, if not downright Biblical. A story that leverages pure symbolism in its attempt to go so much further beyond our shared understanding of the hubris of humanity that it can really only be described as "a mind-job."

That story is *Neon Genesis Evangelion*, and that dad is Gendo Ikari.

Evangelion[1] is an anime series created in 1995, written and directed by Hideaki Anno. It is, among other things, about giant robots[2] fighting Old Testament–style angels (as in eldritch, non-human angels with four faces and six wings, made of living metal) to try and stop a third Biblical apocalypse in

---

1. Which I will shortly truncate to *Eva*.
2. That aren't really robots.

Neo-Tokyo. The protagonist is a young teen named Shinji Ikari. Shinji's one of the vanishingly few people who can pilot one of those Earth-saving robots. His dad, Gendo, runs NERV, an NGO tasked with keeping those robots up and running. That's where *Eva* starts, and then it gets weird. I'm talking clones. I'm talking the nature of identity. I'm talking deep, deep depression where the protagonist can't get out of bed for a few episodes, despite the fact that he is, quite literally, the only person who can save the planet. I'm talking melon farming as the world burns. Powerful references to Schopenhauer and Freud in what is supposed to be a kids' show about saving the world from "aliens." Oh yeah, and something called the Human Instrumentality Project.

Japanese animation godfather/wizard Hayao Miyazaki[1] worked with Hideaki Anno back in the day,[2] and in the documentary *The Kingdom of Dreams and Madness,* Miyazaki said that Anno was a weird guy. His proof was that Anno sat in his office chair cross-legged. "Who does that?" Miyazaki said, with elfin glee.

In its original twenty-six-episode run, *Eva* falls apart. Not, like, "Oh the show loses steam," but rather the form meets the content head-on. What starts out as a genre tale of robots punching aliens with power-knives shifts, episode to episode, into the anxiety at the root of our identities. The show posits an "AT Field," a kind of metaphysical barrier that maintains personhood via individuation. The only way to destroy an angel is to somehow pierce this field. That metaphorical field is compared to Schopenhauer's Hedgehog Dilemma: we

---

1. The creative genius behind Studio Ghibli's *Spirited Away, Princess Mononoke, My Neighbour Totoro,* and many other classics. A fairly Distant Driven Dad bod, too, now that I think about it …

2. Anno was an animation lead on one of Miyazaki's older films, *Nausicaä of the Valley of the Wind.*

seek to be close to one another, we yearn for contact, yet, because of the nature of consciousness, we have spikes, we hurt one another, and we retract from that pain. How can we be close when clinging pierces? Must we fall in love with the pain? Must we huddle alone in the cold and the dark? Keying a personality in too much one way or the other leads to any number of psychological breakdowns, of which the author was all too familiar — the pressure of making *Eva* drove Anno to severe clinical depression.

Shinji is a human manifestation of the Hedgehog Dilemma. He's basically an orphan. His mother (Yui) died in the backstory to the show, and his father left him to caretakers and nannies as Gendo went off to save humanity from the angel-aliens. Shinji's been alone his whole life, and because he's never experienced the warmth of human concourse, he only feels the prick of quills — and because his experience oscillates between pain and nothing, that pain is exaggerated to the point of being unbearable.

What's incredible is that the alien-battle parts of *Evangelion* are top-notch. If you're the kind of person who likes meaty grapples with eldritch horrors, then you will dig it. The show doesn't dispense with a straightforward genre narrative for lack of the capacity to do so, but rather because it yearns to tell a bigger story. A story beyond the bounds of robots, aliens, and teenagers.

The urge to tell a story beyond its limitations eventually sees *Eva* break down the conventions of narrative animation itself, diving in the last few episodes into the incoherent, surreal internal worlds of the protagonists' identity structures and collapsing memory as the angels finally destroy mankind's last bastion of resistance.

What does all of this have to do with Gendo? Well, he is the character who most mirrors the overall arc of the show, despite his limited screen time and our extremely restricted insight into his internal world.

He, too, wasn't happy with the status quo. Gendo Ikari was tasked with the relatively straightforward job of "defeat those aliens" and "stop another apocalypse." Instead, by seeing into the heart of these angels and what this new cosmological situation meant, Gendo recognized the nature that the AT Field represented: a space beyond the individual, and thus an opportunity for humanity to transcend the limitation of being a single mind trapped in a stew of meat and bones and nerves.

He was thinking in the biggest possible perspective. Run this organization? Sure. Cook up some robots that can defend Earth from giant aliens with unknowable powers? You got it. Build an underground fortress to house humanity? No problem. How about he goes to the root of the problem: The fact that no human mind can perfectly interface with another?

Now he's going after the root of all suffering.

Or at least that's what he thinks. See, like all Distant Driven Dads, he is conflating his own suffering with that of humanity's. Unknown to this dad bod, some folks *actually like* being people. That is a thought that literally has not crossed Gendo's mind, or if it has, he's dismissed it as an illusion or mistake.

The pragmatic details of running a world-saving organization are more than enough to punt Gendo into the same distant territory as Dr. Jones Sr.: he's just too busy to spend any time with his kid. However, the relative believability of that total abnegation of a relationship with his son is a whole lot higher because of the existential stakes of *Eva*: this guy is the only scientist on the planet who can run this show and humanity is racing against the clock. There is no time to change diapers or hold hands on the first day to kindergarten.

This distance creates an image in Shinji's mind of his father as this stern, remote taskmaster. He is unable to voice his true feelings of neglect and pain — so instead he parrots what seems like the right thing to say in the circumstances, initially claiming he is proud of his dad. It's only once block after mental block is removed through the psychic pain of piloting these gigantic organic robots (that break down mental barriers in his mind just like the AT Fields break down the metaphysical barrier between entities) that Shinji can admit just how much pain he is in for want of his father's affection.

When we see them interact throughout the show, Gendo's always telling Shinji what to do, like any other employee of NERV. He treats his son coldly, doesn't reward him with a hug when his little boy saves the day, and a big chunk of fuel for Shinji's breakdown and abandonment of the whole "save the world" project is that doing so doesn't contribute to his unconscious wish that it'll bring him closer to his dad.

That is one cold tony.

Turns out, Gendo didn't want to save the world. He wanted to transform it. By harnessing the aliens' power and bringing about the apocalypse, he causes the mind of every sentient being to collapse into a singularity. Also, their physical bodies become goo, further reinforcing the idea that individuation is unnecessary when we can all become primordial soup together.

This was Gendo's goal all along, to leverage the angels and transform humanity into a kind of god-being, so that he could get back with his wife again. She'd be in there, you see, because her mind was trapped inside the giant organic robot Shinji was piloting — they'd recorded it in there a few days before she died. Once everyone souped up and all souls[1] were stirred together and coalesced into some new state of existence, he'd be back with Yui.

---

1. Spirits, minds, whatever. Take your pick of astral metaphors.

So the universal "end all suffering" and the personal "end my suffering" collapse, just like the AT Fields that keep us from truly connecting beyond the gulf of void between human minds.

In the ultimate sci-fi contradiction, to hold to that impossible goal meant that Gendo held himself separate from his son, the last vestige of his wife left to him. Instead, he kept cloning her, over and over, as a teenager — which is pretty gross![1] In the end, reconnected for a brief moment before Shinji restarts history by maintaining his individuality,[2] Yui lets Gendo know he done messed up. She didn't want this. She would've preferred he be a good dad and, you know, love their kid rather than force him to relive the horrors both of them endured in the previous apocalypse, over and over again, each time Shinji destroyed an angel.

Like all Distant Driven Dad bods, Gendo has power. Unfortunately, rather than using that power to help others, he uses it to shape the world in his image, mistaking himself for God. He doesn't even just choose suicide. He instead performs genocide, confusing the entire world for manifestations of his own suffering.

Dude needs a serious reality check.

·

These Distant Driven Dads are their own worst enemies. They set themselves up for failure by defining their ambition and their prerogative as "Me vs. the World." That forces their children to choose: be a graft of my father's will, or be his enemy. Of course, any individual worth their salt is going to end up on

---

1. Maybe I should've mentioned that earlier.

2. Which is actually pretty heroic. He chooses potential pain, despite the fact that it completely floors him, in order to not abnegate individuality. Thanks, bud.

the side of "the world," whether or not they have any particularly strong feelings about it.

Through this obsession with control, with an overwhelming need to assert, to define on behalf of others the frame of the argument, the Distant Driven Dad bod eventually places everyone and everything on the side of "the world." Which makes sense, it's the world! It's everything! In so doing, by placing himself in opposition to existence, the Distant Driven Dad loses control over any and everything. So utterly disconnected, he has no influence, which would come instead from understanding and integration, rather than brute manipulation.

Sometimes these dads get lucky, and they outsmart everyone and beat "the world." Of course, as soon as they've done that, they've lost. Whether or not they realize it. No matter how grand their illusions or their ego, it turns out each and every one of these jerks is just a shade of *Citizen Kane*. Someone demanding love and tribute, without knowing how to give it in return.

When you beat the world into submission, it turns out there's nobody left to control but yourself.

Major Dad

THE MILITARISTIC FATHER ARCHETYPE, all haircut and discipline, seems like it ought to be a proponent of only the most regressive parental policies. Generally, this'd be true. The military dad next door in *American Beauty*, Frank Fitts (played by Chris Cooper), is a great example of this archetype: on the outside he's a hard-as-nails, homophobic fetishizer of fascism and an extremely strict father who sends his son to military school rather than celebrate his weird little videos about grocery bags. The fact that this Major Dad persona merely papers over the contradiction of a self-hating gay guy (or, to be a titch more charitable, a man who has been conditioned to not accept queerness in any form, despising it within himself, and fixating on it externally) is a unique twist to the norm. But it's that stern outer body that we're really interested in here.

Military discipline, as it was described to me by my grandfather (who served in the Korean War), is all about the elimination of idiosyncrasy. You need to be able to move as a unit, instantly, without thought or doubt getting in the way. When your sergeant yells "Down!" you need to be down. Any perturbation or misapprehension in that organic whole made up of multiple bodies means bad news. Not just for you, but for your entire squad. If the enemy sees one of you, well, then they're going to bomb that entire area.

This "one for all" mentality exists in the ritual of military as well, where a self-reinforcing emergent collective justice bends individualism out of the picture from the get-go. Say someone doesn't do the right thing in a squad during boot camp. Too slow, not responding with the right salute, talking out of turn, whatever — *everyone* does push-ups. Sure, it's not fair, but it's effective. After everyone else has to do push-ups because ole Bob is messing up, Bob's squad mates are going to make sure that Bob doesn't mess up again. In sunnier war flicks, they band together to help Bob overcome his weakness and become a contributing member to the team. In darker ones, he is bullied into coherence.[1] Either way, the unit wins, and the nail that stands up is hammered down to join the rest.

•

Military dads may seem trivially obvious as a dad bod, an archetype both old and well-beaten like an expired pony. Sadly, this bizarre, conformist behaviour that stems from military culture is still quite prevalent in the real world of boys.

Whether it's uncles making homophobic jokes at their nephew's expense, dads picking on perceived oddities in their son's behaviour, or gangs of male friends ripping on each other's mild flaws or out-group eccentricities.

I'm always shocked by this one. Either blunt and obvious or subtle and passive-aggressive, almost every collective of men I've witnessed exhibits this style of conformist ribbing. It's a form of dominance display that mirrors the constant

---

1. Or suicide.

competition at the heart of adolescent masculine identity formation. That "can't you take a joke" type of bullying that is one of the many tendrils of toxic masculinity.[1]

Maybe I can't. I never quite understood the antics of the locker room, which, back in my day, meant mooning the teacher, hitting someone else's penis as they urinated, or doing an ostentatious striptease in the middle of the room and calling anyone who looked up a well-known homophobic slur. It was always the most physically mature guys who participated in this behaviour. The rest of us with our eyes downcast, shovelling on our pants as quickly as we could.[2]

The result of this ubiquitous performance of male dominance, and its corollary battening of emotional expression, is explored (among many other aspects of male isolation) in painstaking detail in my bud Stephen Thomas's 2017 essay "The Legion Lonely."[3] Citing developmental psychologist Niobe Way, who interviewed thousands of boys in her book *Deep Secrets*, Thomas outlines the general trend line of boys *actually* having deep friendships as children and early adolescents. What's more, they aren't afraid to express their love for their friends, or how amazing it is that two people can truly understand one another.

Then a stark shift occurs between the ages of fifteen to twenty, where boys not only lose actual friends, but also their trust in the idea of friendship, via betrayal at the hands of those they thought had their back. During that same age gap, boys adopt "display rules" about what kinds of behaviour they're allowed to show. This disavows expressions of hurt, worry, care

---

1. Its core tenets being social dominance, misogyny, homophobia, the normalization of violence and bullying, and the big one: emotional repression.

2. Oh man, every time my toes got caught in my underwear I died twice.

3. Stephen Thomas, "The Legion Lonely," *Hazlitt*, August 11, 2017, hazlitt.net /longreads/legion-lonely.

or concern for others, and self-conscious emotions like shame or embarrassment.

The power of this panopticon of conformity among men self-reinforcing the status quo of militaristic masculinity is startling in its ubiquity. It starts young, and it sticks around.

•

Curiously, going back to some of the top-line items of the militaristic model — discipline, developing grit, self-control, resilience — none of those are problems in and of themselves. In fact, contemporary parenting books and child psychology have taken a bit of a reroute through the realm of emotional well-being, centring it on the ability of parents to help children train their resilience, like a character stat in a video game.

I shouldn't poke fun. It's predicated on the growth mindset,[1] the fundamental insight that we aren't stuck with a predefined set of personal skills but can, instead, modify ourselves to grow beyond our current capabilities. This is as true of our ability to withstand hardship as it is for our capacity to communicate effectively or be aware of how our emotions are impacting ourselves and others.

With hard work, awareness, and the *idea* that growth is possible, comes the ability to widen our window of capacity or tolerance, depending on the skill in question.

I generally agree with the value of this perspective, but I'm left scratching my head when I try to imagine a model that takes the good parts of the Major Dad bod while leaving the rest behind. Does such a disciplined, authority-coded male father figure exist without being overbearing? Someone equally interested in and somehow balancing the internal needs of

---

1. Carol Dweck's very cool idea from her 2006 book *Mindset: The New Psychology of Success*, which suggests that we can train and develop abilities and character traits previously believed to be set in stone, like empathy or resilience.

self-actualization alongside the external needs of conformist society? A kind of Stoic philosopher-dad, integrating these two roles rather than (as I tend to do, and as I think we tend to do in our culture) simplistically setting them up as a duality?

I'm gonna have to dig deep here. Self-actualized dad bods, or even those that give lip service to a stoic balance of philosophical concerns, are few and far between. Dredging through the media that's touched my life gives me one solid candidate: Calvin's Dad. This is a big one for me. Bill Watterson's *Calvin and Hobbes* was a childhood treasure that I discovered because my parents left the comics lying around the house.[1] For those who don't know, *Calvin and Hobbes* was a daily comic strip about a little boy with no friends except for his stuffed tiger, who he imagines to be a philosophically astute, living jungle cat. Calvin is a precocious, mischievous, and adventurous little boy who has a terrible time fitting in.

Calvin's Dad is unique among dad bods in that I think he is the only one who doesn't have a proper name. He is portrayed throughout *Calvin and Hobbes*'s ten-year run not from Calvin's point of view, but almost always in reference to his role *as Calvin's Dad*. What I mean is, he does not have a life that we experience outside of being Calvin's Dad, even though we catch glimpses of that life all the time through the exchanges that he does have within the family home.

Same with Calvin's Mom.

Calvin's parents are also unique among pop culture fictional parents in that they carry a significant weight and verisimilitude despite this incredibly keyhole view into their internal

---

1. So many of my best childhood art experiences were found rooting through my parents' stuff. They felt like real discoveries, despite being curated (either implicitly or explicitly).

lives. They are seen both from the perspective of and in relation to their son, and yet there are so many other telltale bits and bobs that they mention as they go that you can tell these are really interesting people who would be great to have as guests to a dinner party, if only they could concentrate long enough to carry on a conversation rather than be worried about what their son was going to do to the babysitter.

Like: Calvin's parents mention Thoreau off the cuff. They have Karl Marx and Immanuel Kant on their bookshelf. They try to live with humility and respect. They are damn good to each other. They think things through. They try to steer their son away from violence, away from television, away from unhealthy choices. They connect to the bigger picture and try to approach life at least a little philosophically, attempting to do their best *as people* as well *as parents*. They read up on child psychology books and do the homework when they are trying to figure out what is going on with their son. They read in front of their kid, frequently, which is shown to be a great behaviour to model. They stay up late to do the work so that they have more time with their kid. They put special thought into the activities that they do together as a family,[1] as well as putting thought into the basic, fundamental day-to-day chores that their son is whimsically incapable of appreciating — and they do it for him regardless of the fact that raising Calvin is an almost thankless task.

They are really quite good basic models for parenting. All of the normal things you have to do as a parent, they just do them. They don't complain, because they understand that this is the covenant they signed up for. And even though there are a number of sexist hangovers in terms of the division of labour

---

1. Like, if the comic came out after 2010 they would absolutely be going to farmers' markets.

in the household, there is mention of that, in that wry turn-of-the-century way that people would comment on how unfair it was that Dad left Mom the dishes *again*, but he still didn't step up, you know? So it's a telegraph in the right direction, without quite being a step.

What's crazy about Calvin's Dad is that despite coding totally Liberal Suburban Lawyer,[1] he is absolutely a wannabe Major Dad authority figure. *So many* of his exchanges with Calvin involve directly telling his son what to do, whether it's eating dinner or not watching television. Sometimes, in gems of comics that stand out like emotional spikes in a sea of childhood whimsy, he plays with Calvin or talks to Calvin about something that they both find interesting, but the vast majority of their relationship is one of opposition and authority. Calvin seeks to undermine his father's authority at every step, often resulting in, well, the drill sergeant's core tactic: yelling.

Thankfully violence is[2] not present in the series, which ran from 1985 to 1995, a time when the debate around corporal punishment for children was closer to fifty-fifty than it is now.[3]

Anyway, the primary correspondence between Calvin's Dad and the Major Dad archetype is the focus on specific traits and attributes that Calvin's Dad seeks to instill in his son, by hook or by crook. See, Calvin's Dad is obsessed with "Building Character," a term that is purposefully left vague throughout the comic strip (in order for it to be funnier when it shows up, but also because any middle-aged man's hobby horse is a shape-shifter of remarkable adroitness, a lens through which almost any hot-button topic can be interpreted, and a tool that

---

1. Calvin's Dad's great personal pastime is cycling to work.

2. Almost. There's definitely references to off-screen spanking, which is unfortunate.

3. Aw, Christ, I actually looked up the stats on spanking. Damn they're depressing. Why did I do that to myself? Sorry. I need to take a quick break …

can be used on a downright shocking number of situations) but basically means developing the traits that help an individual conform to society and "succeed" in terms of the external measures of success in North America: getting along with others, putting up with hardship, or doing the work you need to do even (perhaps especially) when you really don't want to.[1]

Calvin's Dad wants Calvin to, if not quite fit in, at the very least *pass* for fitting in, and be able to get through the day with a bit more of an acceptance of communal values and a bit less zany reordering of priorities. It's important to remember: Calvin is an unapologetic weirdo. His best friend is an imaginary tiger. He spends more of his time in worlds of make-believe than he does in the real world, and his value system almost totally coheres to the principles of discovery and wonder rather than anything even remotely pragmatic.

You get the sense throughout the series that Calvin has never had a group of friends, and thus is simultaneously a bit tragic but also kind of immune to the peer pressure that the militaristic model of emergent, conformist group discipline relies upon. Calvin is like that old Wittgenstein[2] quote about being alone despite being surrounded by people who don't get you; in cases like that you have to manufacture your own oxygen.

Much to Calvin's Dad's chagrin, any appeal to authority falls flat to Calvin's ears. This is especially damning as an engine of their relationship because, while it makes for great daily

---

1. Thankfully, in the newer models of grit, inspired by psychologist and author of *Grit*, Angela Duckworth, there are also internal measures of "success" such as happiness, well-being, balance, and the like. Even though they're pretty bland earmarks, I'm glad that popular psychology has caught up to the obvious.

2. Ludwig Wittgenstein. Hyper-influential Cambridge philosopher from the early twentieth century. Obsessed with logic, language, and the ineffable. A total weirdo who was most definitely a loner. After giving away his family's Rockefeller-level fortune after the First World War, dude built a cabin on a remote Norwegian cliff where he had to row, by hand, to the nearest settlement. Google him if you want to check out other awesome, eccentric anecdotes.

strip content, it means that they can never really advance beyond the cut and thrust of witty repartee.

This is a little sad because Calvin's Dad doesn't just want his son to conform for the sake of conforming; he honestly seems to believe that this will make Calvin happier in the long run. That attention paid to cultivating these qualities will help his son become a more well-rounded person. Of course, Calvin's six years old, so there's plenty of time for that throughout the rest of his life, but the freeze-frame anti-chronological nature of the comic strip means that, like Charlie Brown, he is confined to his initial description.

So any exploration of this theme falls a little flat. It's there, a tension between Calvin and his dad, but the only resolution that we find is provisional to the punchline of a particular comic strip. It doesn't build in complexity over time, especially in comparison to the many other themes that Watterson explored, or the raw artistic virtuosity he exhibited in those Sunday panel spreads.

In this way, Calvin's Dad is a bit of a teaser. Despite being an incredibly grounded father figure in and of himself, and one of the most solid dad bods out there,[1] the parts of Calvin's Dad that relate to militaristic authority and the need to balance philosophical internal growth with external conformity are an appetizer at best.

·

A much more fulsome example would be Major Garland Briggs,[2] the father of Bobby Briggs,[3] from David Lynch and

---

1. Seriously, when it comes to everyday parent models, I think about Calvin's parents more than almost any other fictional characters. They take up exactly as much of my mental space as my friend's parents from when I was growing up.

2. Played by Don S. Davis.

3. Played by Dana Ashbrook.

Mark Frost's mystery-horror TV show, *Twin Peaks*. *Twin Peaks* aired from 1990 to 1991, pretty much the same time period as *Calvin and Hobbes*, right in the middle of the comic strip's tenure. They're speaking to the same America, over the newspaper and the television set.[1]

Despite that, as nutty as referencing *The Communist Manifesto* is in a comic strip, and as surreal as Calvin's make-believe adventures were, because they were confined to the drawn panels of a comic strip, they had less uncanny punch than *Twin Peaks*, which wore its Lynchian madness on its sleeve and provided an atmosphere far more permeable and frightening. Like a nightmare compared to a daydream.

In neither would I expect to find a soulful recalibration of the father figure, and yet Major Garland Briggs is exactly that.

I won't bother setting up the whole show, since a sketch will suffice. The horrendous murder of Laura Palmer shocks a small town, and the outsider[2] sent to investigate unravels the seamy network of decadence and rot that lies just beneath the surface of this seemingly perfect slice of small-town America.[3]

Thematically, early *Twin Peaks* is all about that dark disconnect inherent to the American communal project. How something pretty and picturesque on the surface is disgusting and violent underneath. Like a prom queen who's secretly a drug addict and prostitute that delights in depravation as a result of childhood trauma, that sort of thing. The lies we tell ourselves so we can sleep at night. The chemicals we use to still the howling mind. The wounds we wreak on those we love by simply being broken little creatures in an imperfect world.

---

1. Two formats of mass media that enjoyed an incredible stranglehold over people's attention at the time.

2. FBI special agent Dale Cooper, played by national treasure Kyle MacLachlan.

3. There is, of course, a hell of a lot more than that, but I want to get to Major Briggs.

It's the kind of story where there is very little room for intelligent goodness. More often, good is a kind of goofy puppy dog, bouncing around from plot point to plot point in an entertaining way. Sniffing its way along the scent of corruption.

Bobby Briggs was Laura Palmer's boyfriend. He was the football captain, and an arrogant jock to boot. He dabbled in selling drugs at high school by working for Leo Johnson, the local ponytailed dangerous backwoods connection to the drug trade. Apparently, Laura got Bobby into it. On the side, Bobby was having an affair with Shelly Johnson, Leo's wife who worked at the Double R Diner — the diner being basically the heart of the town of Twin Peaks.

Bobby is a hooligan. Upon Laura's death, his grief takes the form of increased acts of desperate shenanigans: threatening Laura's, uh, other boyfriend, James; playing a dangerous game of cat and mouse with Leo; and generally being a smart-mouthed layabout.

Bobby's dad, Major Briggs, comes off at first almost like comic relief. He is so gruff, so formal that I thought this guy was the exterior-conformist Major Dad *and nothing else*. It really seemed like he had nothing going on inside whatsoever. Oh, how dad bods can deceive.

In his very first exchange with Bobby (helping out with his interrogation at the police station after Laura's death) Major Briggs says, "Robert, I'll be at home this evening if you need a sympathetic ear." So direct the emotional offering, so bald, it almost makes sense that Bobby, shouldering the heavy leather jacket of crap teenage masculinity, cannot accept it. Especially in front of the other people present in the scene. "I don't need any damn sympathetic anything," he says, leaving the station.

So the Major tries again, this time in their home, away from the prying eyes of society, to give his son (who's a slouching jerk that backtalks his mother) an opportunity to vent, to express, anything to try and crack that shell. And it's ... it's an incredible slice of self-aware fathering:[1]

> *Robert, I was hoping we would have the chance to discuss the events of the past few days. Not necessarily the physical events themselves, but rather the thoughts and feelings surrounding them. Rebellion in a young man your age is a necessary fact of life. Candidly, a sign of strength. In other words, Robert, I respect your rebellious nature. However, being your father, I am obligated to contain that fire of contrariness within the bounds established by society as well as those within our own family structure.*

During this, frankly, stunning speech that lays out the role of father-as-authority *and* an emotional awareness of the pragmatic reality of being a punk-ass kid, Bobby sits there, totally unengaged. Either he's heard it all before (which is nuts! Why isn't every television dad giving speeches like this?[2]) or he's just so tuned out from his own arrogance that even this slice of pure wisdom falls on deaf ears.

The Major starts to panic, a little, as his well-oiled speech dissipates into panicky stoic aphorisms:

> *Robert, I note your reluctance to enter into a dialogue with me, your father. There are times when silence is golden. Silence can be taken many ways. As a sign of intelligence: the quieter we become, the more we hear.*

---

1. Taken in its entirety from *Twin Peaks*, "Episode 1."

2. Because it demands a level of forethought common mortals have no access to in the everyday insanity of raising a family.

Bobby puts a cigarette in his mouth and glares at his dad with the droopiest rebel-eyes I've ever seen. Major Briggs slaps the smoke right out of his son's petulant lips. Bobby is stunned.

Now, I am a tolerant man, but my patience has its limits.
"To have his path made clear is the aspiration of every human being in our clouded and tempestuous existence."[1] Robert, you and I are going to work to make yours real clear.

Bobby's mom, Betty, delicately plucks the cigarette from her meatloaf and tries to smile supportively. "We're here for you, Bobby."

Bobby smiles a befuddled half-smile. Part smirk, part disbelief, part arrogance reasserted.

The amazing thing is, despite everything else going on in Twin Peaks, the Briggses follow through. They take their son to family counselling, which is exactly the right course of action given the circumstances. They follow the psychiatrist's advice and allow Bobby to see him one-on-one, which leads to a breakthrough.

It isn't everything, mind you, it doesn't solve Bobby's behaviour or help him with his "sleeping with the wife of your drug-dealer boss" problems, but as a model of fathering, slap aside, it's pretty great. You've got a frank discussion of emotions, the desire to begin a dialogue, the expression of respect for your rebellious child's actions, at least in the abstract, and an earnest attempt to work through the issues with them — to give them the help they need, even when it isn't the help you think they need. It's important to note that Betty and the major are initially reluctant for Bobby to meet with the psychiatrist alone — they want to work on this together, as a family — but

---

1. Quoting Joseph Conrad at the dinner table.

they also recognize the paramount need for Bobby to figure this out on his own, or else he will never be able to manage adulthood.

Then the show cranks up a notch. In classic soap-opera style, events in the sleepy town of Twin Peaks ratchet up in intensity every episode, until Bobby's almost been axed by Leo, he's seen Leo get shot, and Shelly's nearly died in a fire at the old sawmill. In comparison to the melodramatic hijinks of the show, Major Briggs's attempts to be a solid dad seem quaint. However, if you take them out of context and inspect them for what they are, acts of parental devotion and love, despite being way over the top, I still find them incredibly valuable and affirming.

The next time Bobby and Major Briggs really meet is at the diner,[1] Twin Peaks's communal hub and sanctuary. Bobby is again slouching beneath the weight of his torrid existence; the major is enjoying a snack in a booth. Seeing his son, the major asks if Bobby will join him. Bobby assents. Notably the major doesn't ask Bobby if he wants to get into a tête-à-tête about the value of Stoicism versus Epicureanism, he just asks his son to join him.

Despite having something major to share, Major Briggs eases into the metaphysics. "How was school today?" he asks with earnest curiosity. "School? Fine," Bobby says after a theatrical sigh. "That's good," the major says, taking a bite of pie. Then, importantly, he says nothing.

There is a curious phenomenon with my son. Like most toddlers, he is very interested in testing the boundaries of our authority (alongside the boundaries of pretty much everything else). When I forget this and try to go head-to-head with him on the simple necessities of life, such as bathing, brushing his

_____
1. In "Episode 8."

teeth, etc., it never ends well. In opposition we are at logger-heads, and he is so much more capable of stubbornness than I am, because he does not see the need to do anything else beyond what is emotionally right in front of him. He doesn't know about the fact that we need to get him to bed, or that we need to get out the door, or that there are all of these external concerns and considerations that place the toothbrush within a matrix of activities that need to get done in order to dance through the day's logistics. So he can sink right into that act of uncivil disobedience and refuse to co-operate till the cows come home.

If, however, I recognize this and catch it quickly enough, I can suggest that he needs to open his mouth to let me brush his teeth, and let him know that I'd like to do it when he's ready. I can place the badge of power into his hands and, much more often than not, he will think about it and shortly comply. By stepping away from authority, by granting my son agency, I give him the latitude to do what he knows is best, despite the fact that he will never, ever do it if it seems as though I am try-ing to force him directly.

In the scene, Bobby steps into that negative space left in Major Briggs's silence, and he asks his father how his day was at work. The major provides a similarly mundane answer as his son, "Work? Work was good." Bobby sits up, his interest actual-ly piqued. He asks his father what he does exactly, to which the major unfortunately is pledged to respond, "That's classified."

Bobby is stymied, and you can tell he's actually kind of sad that the dialogue seemed like it was going to end at that road-block, that wall of the father's symbolic role as representative of the external world and its structures of power.

Then Major Briggs flips the script again.

He offers his son a piece of pie, which is particularly fresh and particularly delicious, and notes his son's ... I've looked at this face now for a while. Concern? Sadness? Confusion? Lack of direction? Bobby is all of that, and more.[1] He wants to connect, but he doesn't know how. He wants to reconcile, but he cannot do so openly. His situation is so melodramatic, even his gruff but cool and understanding military father couldn't parse it out.

So the major stretches into the cosmic. "Bobby," he says, tentatively, "may I share something with you?" His son assents.

A vision I had in my sleep last night. As distinguished from a dream, which is mere sorting and cataloguing of the day's events by the subconscious. This was a vision. Fresh and clear as a mountain stream. The mind revealing itself to itself.

So far Bobby is not impressed. He's falling back onto the well-worn slouch and relaxed facial features of the teenage hooligan, but the Major presses on.

In my vision, I was on the veranda of a vast estate. A palazzo of some fantastic proportion. There seemed to emanate from it a light from within this gleaming, radiant marble. I'd known this place. I'd in fact been born and raised there. This was my first return. A reunion with the deepest wellsprings of my being.

Bobby reacts to this. He looks thoughtful.

Wandering about I noticed happily that the house had been immaculately maintained. There'd been added a number of additional rooms, but in a way that blended so seamlessly with the original construction, one would never detect any

---

1. Dana Ashbrook really does some work in this scene.

difference. Returning to the house's grand foyer, there came a
knock at the door. My son was standing there.

Bobby looks up. He is within his father's vision, both in the
sense that his dad is talking about, but also, *he can see it.*

He was happy and carefree. Clearly living a life of deep har-
mony and joy. We embraced. A warm and loving embrace,
nothing withheld.

Bobby starts crying.

We were, in this moment, one. My vision ended. I awoke with
a tremendous feeling of optimism and confidence in you and
your future. That was my vision of you.

"Really?" Bobby says, in emotionally charged disbelief. "I'm
so glad to have had this opportunity to share it with you," the
major replies. Bobby is overwhelmed. Rendered speechless by
the frank description of a father's dream for his son. Happiness.
Harmony. The opportunity to embrace, to hold nothing back.
To be together, as one.

Not the "one" of the military unit, sanding off the edges
of difference, but the "one" of two beings fully accepting one
another, faults and foibles and all, sharing a love unconditional.
To live without fear of rejection, and to enable that freedom in
others, is an incredible vision, no matter the bonkers context.

Major Garland Briggs provides a robust and manly version
of emotional expression, in a package so contextually goofy
that it flies under the radar. What parent wouldn't want the
same for their child? To feel that sense of spiritual kinship with
their offspring, and to know, *to know*, that they were going to
be okay in the deepest sense of the word. To have the courage

to share that vision with a child as difficult as Bobby, and to have it connect, is the apogee of Major Briggs's participation in the Twin Peaks saga.

If Calvin's Dad is a cartoon that feels real, then Major Briggs is like real dad insights drawn to cartoony lengths. Each utterance just a little too on the nose, each expression a smidge too poetic to be legit. Like most of David Lynch's creations, there's an uncanny valley to the major's utterances, as though they come from a linguistic reality just off-centre from our own, weirding the tongue to tickle the ear and place us in a position of constant eerie near-dread.

Yet the sentiment, on this one, rings through. The parent as role model and enforcer of society's rules is a real thing, no matter how much I wish I could just be my little boy's bud. My job is more than that. I owe him more than that. Even though I cherish idiosyncrasy and independence, even though I would never want to wish upon him spiritual conformity — even though, ultimately, I would prefer for him to be able to choose his values for himself, like Calvin, he still needs to figure out how to wipe his butt and carry himself in public.

That balance, between conformity and individualism, is what a dad ought to strive for. An awareness and understanding of both, rather than a rigid adherence to the former.

Let's face it, the world, society, it'll do enough hammering down on the nails that stick out. Kids don't need their dads to do that for them.

•

Unfortunately, for the authority-and-discipline-loving military dad, his schtick fails the acid test. For someone seemingly interested in getting shit done and focusing on the hard, pragmatic realities of life, the actual empirical track record of these dads is abysmal. Major Briggs, despite the beauty of that one moment with Bobby,[1] as far as we can judge a tree by the fruit grown, like, man, things did not grow so well.

Maybe I shouldn't be so hard on Bobby. In the long run of *Twin Peaks: The Return* that aired back in 2017, he was one of the few that turned out "all right," having grown up into a deputy of the police force. However, his life seemed a far cry from the deep joy and harmony that his father envisioned, and much more resembled one of Thoreau's dopest tracks, the one about a life lived in quiet desperation.

Either that moment of philosophical clarity did not help, Major Briggs's subsequent disappearance into another dimension unravelled the potential impact a stalwart and doughty father figure like that could impress upon a boy like Bobby, or, heck, maybe becoming a sad cop was the best possible future for ole Robert Briggs.

By the same token, Calvin's Dad is fundamentally impeded from the goal of providing a conforming influence in his son's life. Any attempt that he makes to help Calvin, say, learn to play baseball to fit in with the other boys ultimately serves to drive Calvin away, further into himself, reinforcing the idea that he ought not try to fit in because it is a doomed enterprise and, if we're being frank, the rest of the kids that Calvin meets[2] are straight-up tools. They are mean, cruel little bastards who take every opportunity to belittle and demean Calvin, if not beat the stuffing out of him.

To take this judgment into a more abstract arena, by placing the mantle of society's structure upon their mortal shoulders, these dads, top to bottom, set themselves up for failure. As Major Briggs points out: rebellion is necessary. Rebelling

---

1. That I will, unconsciously, carry with me (unironically) in my dreams for myself, my father, and my son — heck, for my friends and my family, my in-laws and everybody else. It's a great wish.

2. Barring Susie Derkins, the girl in his neighbourhood.

against your dad is *de rigueur* if he props up his position to you (and his authority over you) as an extension of the greater societal complex.

Once a cocksure teenager starts to see the contradictions inherent in either (a) their father's attributes as a supposed avatar, (b) the society's ethic itself, or (c) the products of that ethic,[1] it is exceedingly unlikely that they are going to go sniffing around, looking for some kind of dialogue or compromise that builds understanding that their father was just trying to do his best with the ethical framework that he inherited, or that worked for his generation, or that he thought made sense from the various sources he could cobble together from the culture and individual examples he had imbibed over the years.[2]

No, that teenager's going to throw the baby out with the bathwater. Once these big daddies have set themselves up as the ultimate exemplar of the state's law, an extension of the will of the superego, then the whole edifice has to come crashing down. Not only does this make for spicy father-son conflict the world over, but it also gets in the way of being able to have the very beautiful, powerful moment of connection that Major Briggs describes in his vision.

If fatherhood, or the authority of fatherhood, or the authority that it projects, is based upon a theatre like it is in this militaristic model, then it cannot connect to the child freely, withholding nothing. Like the cheater or the lie, something will always linger at the back of the mind, stopping that connection from jumping the gap between souls.

And both father and child will suffer for it.

---

1. Let me tell you, there are so many holes to choose from, when your perspective is the moral purity of a kid who's never had to fend for themselves in the real world.

2. You know, their own dad bods.

A Litany of Bad Dads

WHEN GEORGE R.R. MARTIN WAS pressed by the press, over and over again, about the kinds of, shall we say, dubious artistic decisions that seemed a bit unseemly for the frequency of their occurrence in *A Song of Ice and Fire*,[1] he tended to rebut with the same set of well-crafted answers.

Mainly they had to do with the line: "Hrrmph, as you know, I'm a bit of a *student of history ...*" At which point in time GRRM[2] would dive off on an entertaining story about some smidgen of history that he's gussied up and exaggerated in the stories, which is easily one of his genius abilities.[3] So I don't know whether or not anyone came at him with a line about how shitty the dad bods are in his books, but I can

---

1. Look, we all call it *Game of Thrones* in our heads. I'm just going to refer to it as *GoT* going forward.

2. Yeah, let's riddle this with acronyms.

3. Another being crafting characters you love to hate, or the ability that *Anatomy of Story* author John Truby calls "the scene weave," where an author bounces between scenes in a way that not only juices the tension but also reveals thematic interconnections via juxtaposition and abstract resonance. GRRM tickles the mind's quilt.

assume it came from the same quest for historical grittiness that fuelled everything else in them.

To wit, GRRM[1] was going after a pretty solid rock 'n' roll trope-riff against the epic fantasy of the '90s. Say what? Yeah, these are actually some pretty old books. The first one came out in frickin' 1996. No fooling. Back then, the biggest dogs on the epic fantasy block were the kinds of stories where … how can I put this directly? The deal is that there was no moral ambiguity. Heck, there was seldom metaphysical ambiguity.

You knew exactly who the good guys were, and you knew exactly who the bad guys were. The good guys were utterly good, concerned almost entirely with external issues. Their flaws were like the kinds of people who say that "perfection-ism" is their worst trait in a job interview. The bad guys were beyond-redemption bad. They weren't even really villains, or people, more like forces of nature that channelled nether-energy from the rotten bowels of the cosmos. Even worse, everyone could pretty easily be split into either camp (or else labelled something innocuous, like "citizen") and it was palpably obvious to everyone inside and outside the story which was which. The inner world or psychological verisimilitude of these characters, good or evil, was a null wasteland, and these categories of identity were immutable.

This is the[2] framework that GRRM was responding to, with his morally ambiguous characters and his tight over-the-shoulder perspective (that led to many twists and turns both psychological and in terms of how every bit of information that we got about the world was filtered through someone's uncon-scious biases and interpretations, how so much information was doled out, bread crumb by delicious bread crumb, to build

---

1. Say it out loud with me, "GRRM!"

2. Slightly exaggerated.

assumptions and then shatter them) and his world full of piss
and shit and sexual violence.

Leaning on that "student of history" staff, GRRM was
pointing to this lusty tale of blood and bones saying, "No way.
None of that good prince and dark lord nonsense. *This* is how
it would *really* go down." And you know what? There's a lot of
sense, there.

So much so that I'd wager the role that *GoT* played in the
genre is, kind of, played out. These days, that gritty, dark style
of epic fantasy is, well, a thread of epic fantasy. Taken to extremes in the grimdark branch of the fantasy publication tree,
or else folded in to the composite body of more general works,
nowadays the idea that you need at least a little psychological
or social/political realism is totally accepted.[1]

Again, that makes sense. Just take kings as a very basic, very
in your face example. Kings are everywhere in the kind of fantasy fiction that GRRM was railing against. Either as mentors
or the protagonist themselves. They were portrayed as being so
great. The best kings. Their people prospered. The land sang
their praises. Flowers smelled better when they walked through
the garden. Terrible in war, obviously, but only against the bad
guy — and always with honour!

In no way, shape, or form is the basic cruelty or violence of
feudal monarchies present in these stories. Hereditary monarchy is apologized for, again and again, with the idea that at
least you can have a "good" king, and when you do then the
whole machine operates awesomely, top to bottom.

Most of this sentiment is a hangover from Arthurian
legend, specifically the first half of any King Arthur saga, when

1. And kind of makes me wonder whether this has any bearing on the renowned difficulty GRRM has in producing more books. The genre current that he was initially
swimming against is no longer there, and many artists find themselves defined
more by what they stand in opposition to rather than what they stand for.

the king and the country are tied together in a mystic pact. The second half of the King Arthur stories, where everything goes to rot after Arthur sires an incestuous bastard, loses Guinevere to Lancelot, and generally concedes his authority by being well-known as Camelot's court cuckold (all of which plays up the insane political-theological aspect of the story: If a king is God's representation on Earth,[1] is it ever not-blasphemy to act against the king? Messy!) is pretty much ignored.

Instead, like I said, we get the apologia of the "good" king. The fact that a king is a tyrant by definition is nowhere to be seen. Or that the position roots itself in a cascade of what we would probably consider abuses of power, but back then were the levers of power. I don't mean the nutsy sadomasochism and constant needless warfare that makes up *GoT*, that's all pretty heavily exaggerated (which makes sense, right? GRRM[2] is trying to make a point here, and needed to do so loudly and directly given the state of 1995 epic fantasy). Mostly what I mean is the kind of details like, you know, the fact that most warfare at the time was conducted using guerilla raids on other kingdoms' farmlands. Stealing cows and burning crops (but seldom villages) was the preferred methodology, rather than standing in a line and bashing away on each other's armour.

Eliminating not the peasants, necessarily, but the peasants' means of production (so, okay, indirectly they starve to death) was a surefire way of disrupting the economy of your enemy. Then, after a few seasons of campaigning in this manner, once you've got them holed up inside a castle (if you have enough manpower to siege it) *then* you start to bash them over the head.

---

1. One of the roots of the similar connection between father and society we've seen in other dad bods.
2. "GRRM!"

Or, heck, take castles. We think of them as places of protection. Flip it around. They protected the bureaucratic class and served as stations of taxation and occupation of the populace. The castle loomed overtop of regular people, reminding them of the power of the lord and the fact that they could never usurp him. They were staging grounds for "lightning raids" against either the enemy (which was, at best, a patchwork of other gangs of strongmen) or to keep tabs on your own corral of mounted bushwhackers.

So, yeah, pretty different from shining kings with magic swords saving the day.

That's the kind of dirty picture of medieval fantasy that GRRM wanted to bring to the table. And, like I said above, that is a cool project. Nineteen ninety-five me definitely agreed with it, as I was equally bored out of my skull with the fancy lords in bright white armour parading around as though good was a colour of shirt that you wore and little else.[1]

Also, as I mentioned, it makes sense that he had to go a bit overboard in order to sell the image. He didn't just want to paint the floor with dirt, he wanted the dirt to get right up there into your mouth and your nose, so that you would never forget the association of filth to medieval times.[2]

Hence the political instability so crazy, no one could ever rule there (as the vassals would overthrow the monarch in an instant), hence the rampant sexualized violence, the mistreatment (but at least portrayal) of the underclass, the absurdity of the wars, and the complex psychological greyness at the heart of every single character.

---

1. Oh, right. Of course. All of this is probably based on cowboys. Black hats. White hats. Moral purity despite an economy predicated on colonial violence.

2. No, not the dinner theatre.

The side effect, though, is that once lopped out of that divine channel, without the Arthurian model of comparing oneself to the big deity, the dads became, one and all, absolute dog-shit terrible.

•

Let's start with Ned Stark. If a dad's job is, at least in part, to help prepare his kids for the world, then Ned gets a solid C-plus. He covered bows and arrows and swords, for the most part, but completely neglected to inform his children about the actual apparatus of power in the world that they inhabited. They have very little understanding of the intricacies of vassalage, the importance of housecarls, or the ways to navigate administration of a Westeros economy. What's more, his active decision-making throughout the key plots and intrigues of the story indicates a rigid and severe ideology that blinds him to the real and present danger of any number of threats to his children, friends, and retainers. Bonus marks for hiring a dancing/fencing instructor for Arya and doing half of the right thing with Jon Snow.

•

Robert Baratheon gets a straight super-fail. This old battle-axe could not be a worse dad to his blond legal-but-not-biological children if he tried. He spends all of his time drinking and yelling and hunting and having sexual dalliances with the hired help. It's crazy to think that this guy was in power as long as he was. I can only assume it's because (a) he had decent help to do the real work and (b) all of the corrupt families were able to do whatever they wanted, so since this sap never got in their way, they didn't feel a pressing need to get rid of him. As the supposed father of the kingdom, boy oh boy, this old beardo is one ignorant figurehead. The state went from dragon-riding

albinos with a flair for mysticism to a hearty frat boy who only
went after the crown because he was a jealous ex-boyfriend. So
sordid. So pathetic. Just a cussing gasbag. Baratheon is a great
way for GRRM to take the piss out of the Arthurian model,
but there isn't even a shred of dad in this bod. I mean, hell, he's
the man who raised Joffrey. Enough said. I'm going to grade
him "Non-complete."

.

Tywin Lannister is a half-step up. He at least gets an F. Tywin
is obsessed with paternity, legacy, the family name, all that jazz.
He's cold and ruthless and does anything to further what he
perceives to be the goals of the family and, given the hereditary
monarchy that exists within Great Houses, I suppose he's the
guy who calls the shots. But, damn, his kids are all so miserable. And they hate him. They hate his guts. They kind of hate
each other, too, but at least they can bond over how much they
hate their scheming, power-starved dad. He sleeps with one
son's ex-lover. He brutally eviscerates any sense of well-being
or confidence that his children eke out for themselves, instead
making them wholly reliant on "the family" for their emotional
fuel. He's a Distant Driven Dad bod par excellence, exhibiting
and perhaps revelling in the malevolence inherent to the fu-
sion of ego with vision at the expense of everyone around him.
"Everything I did, I did it for the family." Sure, T. Just keep
saying that to yourself.

.

The man who would be king, Stannis Baratheon. Guy takes the
sweetest kid in the whole goddamn story (a smart, kind-hearted
girl afflicted with a skin condition that made her a pariah in
this small-minded medieval horror show) and sacrifices her to
his cultist MILF for a better shot at winning a battle? F this

guy. The Onion Knight is a better dad than Stannis ever was. Seriously, who sacrifices their own kid to win a battle? Try buying more soldiers next time, Stannis. Good riddance. Hard F.

Roose Bolton. What a piece of work. This guy's claim to fame is that he is an asshole, he tortures his enemies, and his son is a sociopath's sociopath. Engineer of the Red Wedding, turncoat, all around cold and calculating jerk who tortures people … not even for kicks. He has no emotions. He just does it to impress upon people how cold he is. They don't call his house "Dreadfort" for no reason. Heck, if anyone sounds like they're stanning for the kinds of dark lords present in the books GRRM was lampooning, Roose is your man. Only a truly deranged monster could have thought raising Ramsey was a good idea. F-minus-minus.

Oberyn Martell. Okay, I have a hard time saying anything bad about Oberyn. His entrance scene alone is worth an entire grade rank. What's cool about him as a father is that he has a bunch of kids from a bunch of different mothers, and he seems to have treated them all well enough that they are fiercely loyal to his memory. The fact that he could see beyond class distinction, and had enough independence of thought to raise his daughters as competent individuals in a ruthlessly sexist imaginary world is also worth at least one gold star. He taught his daughters a bunch of martial abilities, although he seems to have only passed on a medium amount of skulduggery. You know what? I'll give him a passing grade. B-plus for the Red Viper. He saw that little baby and knew it wasn't a monster. Good dad bod feels all around.

Honourable mention: The Hound and Arya. I would watch a whole spinoff show of Arya and the Hound wandering around from one botched attempt to ransom her to another. Their relationship is equal parts mentorship and a kind of prickly odd-couple vibe you get from buddy-cop flicks. The Hound teaches Arya how to survive in the real world, a skill dreadfully missing from her father's education. He's your classic gruff bear of a guy on the outside with a heart of gold, or at least pewter. He tries to overcome his pure-*realpolitik* world view, and succeeds at least in lowering his guard. From a place of trauma, I salute Sandor Clegane, who receives a solid C grade for getting his name wiped off Arya's list.

.

Honourable mention: Samwell Tarly, who tries to be a decent dude and surrogate dad. Takes in a foster kid that his girlfriend had with her dad (not her fault), and does his best to take responsibility for it by bringing her back to his family's holdings and claiming that the kid is his. He tries to set them up with a life, and, despite having received only heaping scorn from his own father, models love and affection for the little kid throughout the brief bit of time we get to see the new family spend together before war, dragons, ice-zombies, etc. throw everything into turmoil. Solid B-minus. Even though we have no idea how well this plan plays out, I think everyone's rooting for Samwell.

.

What's tricky about dadding up *GoT* is that, well, when the world itself is a hellhole that is made a hellhole on purpose by the author, being a decent dad in that space means possessing all kinds of traits that have no bearing on the skills and perspective that are important in our world. So instead, we've got to lean on that ever-present big-dad energy to try to scoop some silver pieces out of this midden of gong farmer dads.

Student of history aside, so many of these dads represent a regressive idea of fatherhood that is very Victorian feeling. They either use their children as pieces in the great game, treat them like some kind of employee, or else are so woefully unprepared to have emotional congress with them that they're more like awkward headmasters than they are dads.

Sadly, any tenderness shared between characters is a bit like sex in an old slasher flick like *Friday the 13th* — it probably means that they're going to die soon, given GRRM's penchant for upending expectations about a character's necessity to the plot.

It's just so many bad dads, one after the other, it makes your head spin. I'm digging through the ole memory banks to find even one solid, warm act of dadly bonding, and I think it'd have to be the in prologue.

You know, the beheading, where Ned is all: "A real king swings his own sword. Executes his own prisoners." That's a proper dad moment in *Game of Thrones*. They sure don't embrace afterward like Major Briggs and Bobby, but there is a transference in that scene. Something like a life lesson that influences Jon Snow's future decision-making and leadership style.

For right or wrong, that tells you an awful lot about the state of dadship in this absolute monster of recent popular culture.

PART THREE:
Tales of Adventure

'Ware the Wanderer

In the marvelous thirteenth-century legend called *La Queste del Saint Graal*, it is told that when the knights of the Round Table set forth, each on his own steed, in quest of the Holy Grail, they departed separately from the castle of King Arthur. "And now each one," we are told, "went the way upon which he had decided, and they set out into the forest at one point and another, there where they saw it to be thickest" (*la ou il la voient plus espesse*); so that each, entering of his own volition, leaving behind the known good company and table of Arthur's towered court, would experience the unknown pathless forest in his own heroic way.

Today the walls and towers of the culture-world that then were in the building are dissolving; and whereas heroes then could set forth of their own will from the known to the unknown, we today, willy-nilly, *must* enter the forest *la ou nos la voions plus espesse*: and, like it or not, the pathless way is the only way now before us.

Out beyond those walls, in the uncharted forest night, where the terrible wind of God blows directly on the questing undefended soul, tangled ways may lead to madness. They may also lead,

however, as one of the greatest poets of the Middle Ages tells, to "all those things that go to make heaven and earth."
— Joseph Campbell, *The Masks of God: Creative Mythology*

PICTURE A GUY, PROBABLY ABOVE average height, on a quest with a child in tow. He's tough, he doesn't say much, but he knows how to take care of shit when it hits the fan. This guy is the apogee of badassery. He's so hard-core, he can dispatch enemies with one hand while the other shields his child's eyes from the ensuing violence. I'm talking about the Adventuring Dad.

Not to be confused with the Dad Going on an Adventure, such as Arnold Schwarzenegger's Colonel John Matrix in *Commando*, whose daughter was kidnapped by a diabolical South American drug lord.[1] Dads like John Matrix are either rescuing their kids, or having secret adventures without them. An Adventuring Dad is raising his kid while having the adventure. The central difference is the child's presence.

Otherwise, the dad is merely falling back into his old habits, his badass persona unshackled from the soft realities of caregiving and the logistics of parenting. He's just another man. *Boring!* Perhaps his motivations are fatherly, and certainly the stakes are higher when your child's life is on the line, but the true wonder of the Adventuring Dad comes from the fact that he's multi-tasking on diametrically opposed planes of action. Changing diapers and punching helicopters. He's a manifestation of a great male power fantasy: I can be a dad and still have fun like I used to. Have your cake and beat it, too.

As an archetype, the adventuring badass with a child gets to multi-task as a character, too. Despite the prescribed lack

---

1. Or Liam Neeson in *Taken*, who is desperately racing against the clock to rescue his daughter from an international human trafficking enterprise.

of male emotional expression permeating pop culture, the Adventuring Dad bod can convey tenderness, care, and affection without actually expressing it explicitly. What I mean is, through watching the dad's macho acts of protecting his ward from harm, the audience still feels the otherwise sublimated emotional concourse between the two characters. This is part of why the child's presence is key, as it unlocks a wealth of emotional expression within the story without demanding that the protagonist alter his stony, stoic mien.

It doesn't even matter if he's a real dad! In *Terminator 2: Judgment Day*, Arnold Schwarzenegger plays Model 101, a robot sent back in time to protect John Connor (Edward Furlong), the leader of humanity's last stand against Skynet, a malicious artificial intelligence with an army of robots. In the timeline of the film, John is a preteen punk, trained by his mother, Sarah Connor (Linda Hamilton), to have the skills necessary to lead the robot wars of the postapocalyptic future. Given that she's *really* focused on that robot war, Sarah's been locked up in a mental hospital, and John bounces around from foster home to foster home. He's ripe for a father figure, and after an initial misunderstanding at the mall (goosed by the fact that Schwarzenegger played the *evil* robot in the first film), he bonds pretty hard with his cybernetic protector.

Throughout the movie, the pair are hunted by an even more advanced robot made out of liquid metal, the T-1000, played by living uncanny valley Robert Patrick. Despite the fact that Model 101 and John barely survive each encounter by the skin of their teeth, Model 101 is never fazed. He's a robot, which plays to Schwarzenegger's strengths as an impossible specimen of muscles and ice-cold killing prowess, but he would be pretty leaden carrying an entire film on his shoulders. John, of course, is losing his marbles. His life got flipped and turned upside down. His mother's postapocalyptic ravings *were true.* John is the locus of emotional expression through-out the movie, his fear, joy, and punk-kid witticisms carrying our catharsis along for a ride. Then, as their bond deepens, and the film stomps and smashes its way toward heroic sacri-fice, the interplay between robot and boy becomes something more like love.

To end the vicious cycle of time-travelling robots, Model 101 has to be destroyed. Otherwise, scientists will reverse-engineer his CPU. So Arnold is lowered into a vat of molten steel, and this robot, who has not expressed a single emotion throughout the entire movie, gives a thumbs-up. Cue the waterworks. John's in tears, I'm in tears, and this Adventuring Dad bod pushed my emotional buttons despite maintaining a cool and frosty de-meanour, entirely due to the presence of the child throughout the action.

The second key male power fantasy bound up in the Adventuring Dad bod is that he's got nothing tying him down or holding him back. With no partner, and no roots, the Adventuring Dad has no reason to compromise or mitigate his violent actions. He can go all out.

This illusion speaks to a dark secret in the heart of many men: They believe they could do more by themselves, without their partners. They would have more freedom, could accom-plish more, could really be themselves, say what they want, do what they want, and get something done around here, if they didn't have to consider anyone else's feelings or the repercus-sions of their actions.

The Adventuring Dad bod provides a venue for this fantasy because of the very nature of adventure: it happens somewhere else. This special mythopoetic space where adventure happens takes on many forms: the Wild West, feudal Japan, Arthurian legend, deep space, the swashbuckling high seas, the Second World War, Middle-earth, etc. What unites these times and places is their capacity for the unsanctioned to occur. Whether social norms are disrupted by war or vast tracts of wilderness, there exists some relationship between order and chaos. There's both a breakdown and some maintenance of order. The adventure takes place among these two states of being, balancing them, oscillating between them, or running away from one, depending on the disposition of the characters.

A great example of this aspect of the Adventuring Dad bod is *Lone Wolf and Cub*, a *jidaigeki*[1] movie series from the '70s where an unstoppable badass samurai, Ogami Ittō, rolls around with his son, Daigorō, in a baby carriage, fending off assassins as he tries to avenge the murder of his wife, Asami, in Tokugawa-era Japan.[2] Right away, the fact that Asami is out of the picture unleashes this guy from the normally rigorous constraints of Japanese etiquette. Ittō was framed for her murder (by the Yagyu ninja clan), and samurai honour dictates that even the *suggestion* that he is guilty means that he ought to commit *seppuku*, ritualized suicide to regain his family's honour. Ittō ain't having none of that. Instead, he grabs his sword and pits himself and his son against his previous employer, the shogun, his armies, and the ninja clan that besmirched his name.

If Asami was still around, then she could take care of Daigorō and the story would revert to Dad Going on an Adventure. At the same time, you can't have a partner in this archetype because discussion, planning, collaboration — that only slows you down. Instead, you need some kind of

---

1. Which literally translates to "period drama," but pretty much means "samurai movie."

2. I mean that quite literally. In the (many) battles that punctuate these movies, Ittō is either locking blades with goons in a deadly dance around his son's wooden UPPAbaby, or else he's lugging his kid in one hand and slashing red ruin with the other.

unquestioned and militaristic chain of command, so that every participant in the drama knows their role and acts within it. Otherwise, you'll get sliced to ribbons. Of course, a child is going to answer to the dreadful need of a warrior. If they don't, the Adventuring Dad will physically intervene. A child's tactical assessment is worthless.

If, on the other hand, Ittō had decided to stay tethered to the status quo of feudal Japan, he'd have offed himself, and we'd have no story at all. To abscond on an adventure demands division from the body politic, standing alone and aloof from social norms, cutting a new ethic from the flesh of those who oppose you. That means Adventuring Dad is, also, a vagabond. A wanderer. Someone who lives on the margins and shifts seamlessly between worlds.

In *Lone Wolf and Cub*, Japan is a war-torn nation trying to rebuild itself, which provides a scaffolding of that tension between order and chaos. That means that there are pockets of anonymity for Ittō to wander through, right until his quest pushes him up against the underlings of his powerful enemies who manage the dominant political infrastructure. So the wandering samurai and his boy skirt the edges of society, living by their own code, pursuing individual goals unrelated to the ethos of their time and place.

On initial distillation, a third key ingredient to the Adventuring Dad bod alchemy emerges: violence is the core skill set that defines masculinity.

It is important to remember the structural rule of action movies: the fights are there for catharsis. There is all of this emotional buildup, via tension and dramatic conflict, and it bursts like a storm with each set piece. The framework is almost beat for beat identical to musicals, except instead of having Schwarzenegger do a bit of soft-shoe alongside a sombre ditty about the shackles of duty, we get a viscera-drenched explosion of choreographed violent activity. Punching is the way men get to express themselves in movies made by and for men.

Both the *Terminator* and *Lone Wolf and Cub* franchises also underscore the need to learn violence in order to survive in the world created by the mythological rubric of adventure. A samurai without a sword is a nonentity. A robot without a gun is dross. The capacity to end another life is the trial through which one must pass in order to have agency within this framework. That's nuts. The constant repetition of this value judgment within these stories aimed squarely at the hearts of men implies, "To be a real man, you need to know how to kill."

•

Fictional violence is ... It's hard to write about sensibly. I mean, it's easy to tap into my own adolescent excitement when it comes to action. I love watching old Jackie Chan films. I love sword fighting. I love the tension and release of violent dramatic catharsis. I love these movies and shows and books and video games. The frisson of that pretend violence is undeniable.

But in my heart I am disquieted by that fact.

My love of fictional violence has been disturbed as of late, by the simple realization that I can enjoy it largely because I have experienced so little real violence myself.

A few years ago, I was lucky enough to write about one of my favourite video games, *Bloodborne*, for a proper international magazine. I had a great relationship with the video games editor, who gave me a lot of leeway within the very tight word count, and I was paid handsomely for my efforts to weave a piece of non-fiction art about gaming.

Bloodborne is, as the name might suggest, a pretty horrific, blood-drenched experience. It is also, pound for pound, one of the best video games ever made. The clarity of its artistic vision, the follow-through by the development team, the way each aspect of the game[1] reinforces the eerie and surreal atmosphere of the imaginary world propagated by systems of dread and nightmare. Just incredible.

A central mechanic, or game loop, involves blasting werewolves and other horrors with quicksilver bullets at *just the right time* so that your character can reach into their innards, grab a handful, and yank *everything* out. Typing that out sounds grotesque. Playing it feels so utterly satisfying. I have a very hard time reconciling the two.

I didn't when I wrote the article. Then, it was pure aesthetic glee.

The day that article was published, something happened on my way home from work. I was walking through Chinatown. It was dark and cold, the last vestiges of winter hanging on to the city like a dirty crust. I saw a crowd gathered in a semicircle around a big Chinese supermarket. The people were watching a fight. Almost casually, it seemed. The guys who hauled the rutabagas were leaning on their pushcarts, cigarettes dangling precariously from their lower lips, too tired or bored or disinterested to get involved. The crowd consisted of shoppers and passersby, old ladies in yellow puffy parkas and office workers like me with techie-looking backpacks and sleek black coats.

Within the semicircle, a rough-looking street-involved white man was pushing and yelling and threatening to punch a middle-aged Chinese guy. The fight was only seconds from descending into blows.

Without thinking I stepped into the ring and slowly, carefully, tried to talk them down. It didn't work, as the middle-aged Chinese guy pushed back at the abuse and things heated up. I

---

1. From the labyrinthine levels to the grotesque enemies, oppressive bosses, sheer difficulty, and obscure storytelling method of providing narrative fragments that the player must piece together on their own.

couldn't get either of them to look at me. I could barely get them to register that I was talking to them. It was only when an older lady joined me in stepping into the fray that they moved away from one another. Everyone dispersed. My heart hurt. From what I could tell from the yelling and the commotion, the fight was about nothing. Or next to nothing.

As far as I knew, the homeless guy was right to be mad. I have no idea what was said or done before I arrived, but because he was the aggressor, I had focused my attention on him.

When I turned to go, the old lady thanked me. She was the one who had done something real and somehow diffused the situation, but she was thanking me for stepping in first, as impotent as my intervention proved.

Something broke inside me as I walked to the streetcar. Something broke and my chest felt heavy. That weight stayed with me for a long, long time. At first, I thought that it meant that my constant[1] appreciation of violent fiction hadn't desensitized me to real violence, because I had such a strong emotional reaction to the threat of the real thing. I thought that it meant there was a strong, thick border between the real and the fictional, and that as long as I kept my attention pointing at the latter, I would be okay and it would not stain my soul in the slightest.

Then I came to realize that the enjoyment I had derived from violent video games and action movies was lessened after this honestly quite simple and low-key incident. It wasn't like I got hurt. It wasn't like someone I knew was injured. It wasn't like I had felt the power of another being who had no care for me as a person and was treating me as an enemy that must be destroyed. It wasn't as though I was forced into a situation where I had to cause harm to another, and live with the disconnect of inflicting injury on another while high on adrenaline.

---

1. It really was constant.

I just broke up a couple of guys who almost started fighting for real.

And still, it messed me up. Even just a little. It was enough that I didn't squirm with glee at the remarkable choreography of an action set piece, and instead found myself wondering why the characters were resorting to violence when there were other options available.

I certainly didn't enjoy reading the published version of my *Bloodborne* review, seeing with perfect clarity the disjunction between those two slices of my self.

Maybe it's just me, but I can enjoy fictional violence a whole lot more when I completely disassociate it from my real life. That ability to disassociate is, in turn, predicated on how lucky I've been to live a life where I've experienced almost zero actual violence.

Which is why violence seems like such a peculiar trait to be so heavily invested in as a gender.

We don't show my son violent media. He has never seen someone die in a film or television show. I don't know how long we can maintain that. I don't even know how to begin having that conversation when he does.

Because the language of film and television, the thrill associated with vicarious action, is a grammar that is built with every show, every cut, every frame. It's embedded in the structure of the media itself. And even though video games can be just as thrilling when they represent abstract geometry,[1] it is a hell of a lot easier to follow Jean-Luc Godard's[2] misquoted advice, and make a story interesting by adding sex and a gun.

Given the prevalence of this grammar, given that I am attempting to speak in this language of our culture, given that

---

1. Such as *Tetris*, one of the best video games of all time.

2. The French new wave film director.

it is so interwoven into the tropes that have informed my masculinity, I have to talk about violence. I have to talk about it honestly: it is incredible and it makes art amazing.

It also terrifies the shit out of me.

It is also embedded in my aesthetic history, making me who I am. Defining, in part, the art I love and, by extension, the art I make. My hope is to maintain that difficult relationship, to carry that Gordian knot, and do so honestly. Rather than paper over the difficulty with empty appreciation or easy outs, accept that this is a living, breathing paradox that informs my own persona.

.

Stepping back into the tired boots of the Adventuring Dad, that necessity for violence is handled in a number of ways, but there is no pretense that it isn't a necessity. It is the tool you need to use to get by in these imaginary worlds. That's why it is so important to remember that these are imaginary worlds, created this way for a reason. Why is violence the way? Why is it so seductive, fictionally, despite being abhorrent in reality?

No doubt I'm bothered about how to approach and understand my love of violent stories, in part, because my kid is two and a half. I can't honestly imagine him at fifteen, period, let alone imagine trying to hold him back from action movies at that age. That would be nuts. But part and parcel of being a parent and venturing into this unknown means that I have accepted the fact that I have no powers of prediction when it comes to the life stages of my little boy. In me, in him, in my wife — every day we are pushing into new territory, every day we are wandering deeper into that unknown wood, together.

It takes up so much bandwidth learning the tools of parenting (alongside, you know, living life) that the idea of tackling an introduction to violent media before I'm forced to is too much. I keep thinking about it in terms of what's appropriate for my toddler, and none of it is. I never want my beautiful, sensitive boy to witness a murder, no matter how fictional. To imagine it feels disgusting. Perverted.

At the same time, when I try to think about what it means that being a man/dad is predicated on enacting violence, I want to retreat to symbols and say, "Nah, what they mean is that the *potential* to enact violence is a symbolic stand-in for the ability to protect." But these movies never lay it out like that, with the cowboy protector looking like he can take care of his own, but actually negotiating a delicate truce with the bandit lord. The way it goes down is one stone cold samurai cuts down the other, and that's how we have our measure of a man: which one is left standing.

This may sound abstract and fantastic, given how seldom you see samurai swords wielded in suburbia, but just take a look at the trailer for Bob Odenkirk's[1] recent sad dad action flick, *Nobody*. Before the movie catapults into unbelievably acrobatic machine-gun wrestling, the set-up is perfectly normal: a sad sack salaryman-looking dad is taken to task by his son, a neighbour, a police officer, and his wife for not intervening physically in a petty home robbery. He had a chance to slug the robber with a golf club, but chose not to. "Did you even take a swing?" the cop asks Odenkirk, whose exhaustion and self-loathing is carved into his face.

Violence was expected, because he was the man of the house. What's more, violence is the sum total of what makes life worth living for this guy who used to be, I don't know, some kind of CIA assassin or something. After taking things into his own hands, he has access to self-esteem again. Instantly his global life-problems go away. His sex appeal goes up with his wife. His son respects him again. He is able to right the wrongs of an

---

1. OMG I love Bob Odenkirk.

unjust world, in a kind of reverse *A History of Violence* where, instead of eroding the life that the escaped-killer-dad built on a mucky foundation of recalibrating his persona from icy-cold to meekly mild,[1] returning to his *Taken*-inspired ways grants Odenkirk an authentically balanced and enjoyable life. So much so that, at the end of the film, he starts doing gigs for the CIA again. Everyone's happy.

Odenkirk's dad character reconnects to the quick of life by killing others. Turns out he was depressed because he wasn't doing what he does best, which just so happens to be bone-crunching, high-octane murder.

Pantomime levels of graphic violence aside, the take-home is the same again and again. A man isn't a real man — a dad isn't a real dad, unless he can pull the trigger.

If not, he's just another victim waiting to happen.

.

You know what? We need to talk about *A History of Violence*, David Cronenberg's action-thriller movie about a dad with a secret. This dad is Tom Stall, played by Viggo Mortensen. As a character, Tom is an ingenious artistic inversion of the Adventuring Dad bod, because adventure comes to Tom, it nearly destroys what makes his life meaningful, and he fights to keep his place in the community rather than disavow it.

Tom owns a diner in small-town Indiana. One day, a pair of crooks try to rob the diner and threaten a server. Tom leaps over the counter and neatly dispatches the robbers, despite the fact that they had guns and he had a coffee pot. Tom's brave stand makes its way onto the news, which blows up Tom's world because, well, it turns out he used to be a gangster in Philadelphia. In fact, he was one of the best, most brutal

---

1. And, of course, all the lies.

killers around. He got out of the game, but wasn't forgotten, and now the mafia are pressuring him to come back to Philly.

This revelation *of course* shatters Tom's family's faith in him as a father. Unlike so many depictions of violent dads, where the capacity to rend flesh is celebrated and glamorized, Tom's family is afraid of him now, and rightfully so! This confusion and terror is translated excellently by Tom's wife, Edie (played by Maria Bello), and his teenage son, Jack (Ashton Holmes), who both still love him, and must wrestle with this newfound monster lurking behind Tom's dewy eyes.

The Jekyll-and-Hyde transformation is even more sinister because small-town Tom is so meek, so gentle. You can tell from his handful of exchanges with staff and customers at the diner that this is the kind of guy everyone loves. The transformation into calculated killer is both instantaneous and absolute — it's another person in there.

This is the terror of *Mrs. Doubtfire* all over again: If Tom could hide *this* from his wife and kids for all these years, *what else* is he hiding? Can he be trusted at all?

At the same time, Jack tries to emulate Tom's behaviour at school, getting into a fight. How can Tom honestly tell his kid that isn't the way we do things? "Oh, so it's okay when you blast a robber's jaw off, but I can't punch a bully at school? Sure, Dad, whatever."

Throughout the film, pressure from Philadelphia eventually forces Tom to go on an adventure, where we see him don the mantle of his former life in order to murder it completely. We, the audience, sees the depredations of Tom's rampage, as well as the adrenal joy that killing brings him. His family doesn't, because unlike the Adventuring Dad, Tom's quest is abnegation of his individualistic past and communion with family and town. He does not want to stand apart, he wants back in to the life he had five minutes before the movie started.

Tom manages to murder his former life in Philadelphia (and anyone who could identify him), thus securing the safety of his family. Then he comes back home. His family's eating dinner. He cannot kill the memories they have of the monstrous acts he's capable of, or the lies he's committed. All he can do is ask for their forgiveness, and attempt to live the truth of his convictions, day after day. He stands at the threshold to the kitchen, bathed in darkness, waiting for a sign from his family.

Silently, Tom's daughter retrieves a plate from the sideboard and places it at Tom's chair. Tom enters the light and sits down. Jack passes his dad some food. Tom is overwhelmed by the offering. Repentance is carved into his skeletal visage. Edie, who has been looking down this entire time, finally looks up at her husband, tears in her eyes. The film ends on Tom, hope kindled if not renewed.

A History of Violence is a great example of the squared circle of artistic slaughter. On the one hand, Cronenberg's tale of a mild-mannered diner owner with a dark Philadelphian past has moments of what I want to call "classic punching," where the audience is provided with opportunities to cheer and applaud the protagonist's heroic martial stand against some straight-up scumbags.

But it doesn't stop there. Most cinematic depictions of violence keep it at the level of conflict resolution and catharsis. Most video games depict violence as *the thing you do* to advance the narrative, or, barring narrative, just *the thing you do*. Every bit of cognitive and emotional feedback comes from reaching out and touching someone in an unpleasant way.

A History of Violence, on the other hand, shows us the ramifications of violence in a bevy of ways. We may applaud Viggo dispatching with diner goons and feel pretty much okay with it, the Western vigilante ethos applying, but can we truly cheer him on when he descends back into the world of the mafia and stomps on a dude's throat? When that barely contained capacity for physical brutality unleashes itself upon the human body, the moral question becomes mired in sticky, opaque fluids. However, it is essentially the same act, one curated for our enjoyment, the other a lingering eye that witnesses the true grotesqueness of a bullet's exit wound.

Then the movie goes one step further. It unpacks, in painful detail, with just as brutal an eye, the lingering social effects of violence upon the protagonist's community, family, and self. The real drama of the film isn't whether or not Viggo Mortensen's secret mafia dad "still has what it takes," which seems like the big question of a film like *Nobody*, but rather: Can we forgive him? "We" as in the community. His family are stand-ins for our moral humanity. We cheer when he performs an act of justifiable violence in protecting them, but then we have to clean up afterward, and the reality sinks in: *he can do this with his bare hands.* Do we want a guy like that in our community? Can we sleep at night with those hands lying right there in bed beside us? Can we trust him with our children?

It's a constant negotiation, both inside and out, and one that is not tied up with a nice little bow by the end of the film.

The amazing thing is that Cronenberg doesn't shy away from the conflict at the heart of this ... conflict. As I noted above, my own uncomfortable conclusion is to hold this paradox rather than try to solve it. Not only does that go against my nature,[1] but it goes against the simple, binary stories we are most often told in mass media. Whether in fiction or in the way news and politics carve bite-sized chunks of meaning for us out of the chaos of reality, they are always easily digestible and have a very clear line in the sand

---

1. I am one of those big-time "you got an emotional problem? Let's SOLVE it" type guys. It is only in the past few years that I've been able to develop the capacity to sit still with ... anything uncomfortable.

between good and evil. Us and Not Us. Never mind the fact that we all know reality is a gosh darn wiggly mess of spaghetti — we still want those easy, patronizing stories. We build our lives out of easy stories.[1]

Even though it's uncomfortable to not solve this conundrum, to not *do* anything with it, that is the way. Violence is attractive, it is also repulsive. We are capable of both. We are both.

Not because we're "men," or fathers, but because we're people.

However, this complicated sitting with the issue, dwelling with the ramifications and realities of violence, simply doesn't seem possible within the confines of the Adventuring Dad bod. It's right there in the name: he ventures, he wanders. After causing untold levels of mayhem to pursue his quest (or whatever), he takes off.

The Adventuring Dad doesn't clean up after himself. He doesn't seek reintegration with society. He takes his ward and moves on to the next patch of anonymity, ready to make the same mistakes all over again[2] and escape by the dint of (in his mind) some alchemy of skill, good fortune, and the cool appraising eye of the nihilist.

The wandering adventurer can only stand against, it seems, never for something worthwhile. They are a corrosive archetype, a clustered paradox, pinballing their way through imaginary worlds of adventure.

Or are they?

---

1. Heck, they even build nations out of these simplistic fables.

2. Okay, now he's sounding a little like a serial monogamist.

Enter Pappas

VIDEO GAMES ARE WEIRD NARRATIVE spaces. So much of the structural asceticism that goes into making novels, movies, plays, and television shows is thrown entirely out the window when it comes to this fledgling medium. In large part, the truly resonant experiences in video games are made up of material that would never make it off the cutting-room floor of a film or a book. They can get away with this, so to speak,[1] in part because the essential interactivity of video games — the foundational fun of pressing buttons and seeing something happen — is predicated on repetition, which is the boogeyman of traditional, or let's say "largely linear," narrative experiences.

We can't really talk earnestly about video game narrative experiences[2] unless we take this Copernican Revolution to

---

1. I admit, I'm not totally sure they're "getting away with it." I'm fairly sure that the difference in narrative scope is a feature, rather than a bug.

2. And we need to, desperately, if we want to say anything relevant about contemporary masculinity, which is so tied up in video games that ignoring it would be tantamount to ignoring military ethos in constructing male identity in the latter half of the twentieth century.

heart. You can analyze a video game as a book, or you can analyze one using the tools of film criticism, and you'll gather some insight — but the text balks, and you feel at least a little guilty, unless you also unpack the way its structured narrative comes into contact with, is buttressed by, or is undermined by the game itself. The buttons that you hit, and the friction that math makes your brain[1] feel.[2]

Math? Yes, math. When you get right down to it, video game design is all about the numbers and how they mesh up with the atmosphere of the art direction. The numbers you see on the screen, and all the invisible numbers that make up the physics of the pocket world you are messing around with while mashing those thick plastic buttons in lizard-brain glee.

Let's feel some math.

•

The best place to start is *Dragon Quest*.[3] *Dragon Quest* is a series of games almost as old as video games being a wide-spread cultural phenomenon. The series creator, Yuji Horii, is sixty-eight years young, and shows no signs of slowing down. *Dragon Quest* games are, for lack of a better word, fairy tales. As with many new forms of artistic expression, video games take old content or tropes and reimagine them in new guises. Every *Dragon Quest* game sees you, the hero, save the world from a dark lord of some sort. At that level, it's basic.[4] But it's the deceptive simplicity of this series that

---

1. And heart.

2. The other central unique element of video game analysis, in my opinion, is atmosphere. The rest can be understood using the tools of film and literary criticism.

3. Released in 1986 on the Famicom, the Japanese version of the Nintendo Entertainment System.

4. GRRM would hate it!

is both (a) a part of its eternal appeal, and (b) why it is such a great place for us to establish the boundaries of this idea that you can feel math.

In the original *Dragon Quest* game, you are literally some random subject[1] that the king asks to save his daughter. You wander around a crayon-coloured world filled with cute monsters designed by shit-hot manga artist Akira Toriyama.[2] Each step in the world has the chance to spring a surprise duel between one of those monsters and you. When you fight a monster, it fights back, and depletes a few of your "hit points," which is a generalized numerical metaphor for how hale you are.[3] You gain experience points,[4] and some gold coins, but lose hit points each battle. In order to not die, every five or so monsters you vanquish, you have to head back to town and sleep in an inn to replenish your hit points. The layers of metaphorical meaning are as thick as a Dagwood sandwich. Resting at an inn could mean literally healing injuries, or maybe chatting with some local townsfolk and taking a day off to rest your weary monster-slaying muscles. The representation is truncated due to the severe graphical and computing limitations, so you have to use your imagination to fill in the blanks.

The nice thing is that the numbers keep on ticking up, to give you a hint of some tangible progress. Staying at the inn costs money, but not as much money as you gain from stomping around the woods slaying enough monsters to *need* a rest

---

1. Okay, you're the ancestor of a hero from legends. So the dad-feels are woven right down into the cribbing on Arthurian myth, here.

2. The guy who made *Dragon Ball*, one of the most celebrated manga series of all time, and an absolute cultural phenomenon when *Dragon Quest* first came out.

3. Derived from *Dungeons & Dragons*, which in turn borrowed the concept from tabletop war-gaming.

4. A similar numerical metaphor for learning.

at the inn.[1] As long as you don't die,[2] you acquire sweet, sweet cash. Save up a hundred gold pieces and you can buy a sword.[3] Now you can dispatch monsters faster, beating ten before you have to go back to the inn. Experience, on the other hand, never goes away. More experience represents character growth: you get a bit stronger, a bit wiser, learn a new magic spell, get a few more hit points as you harden yourself for the journey ahead. In *Dragon Quest* games you can lose money, but not experience. That's a wonderful little life lesson, right there.

In a way, that's the entire game. Go out, look for monsters, take them down, figure out how long you can wander in the woods before you need to recuperate. Eventually you can trek through the wilds long enough to make it to the next town. There you might find a clue about the missing princess, or a lost artifact, or have access to a piece of armour that means — you guessed it — you can fight monsters even longer before coming back home to snooze in the inn and drink away your bites and burn marks.

This is the game loop. And it is essential because the chunks of geography that make up the world in *Dragon Quest* are such that they increase in difficulty, with wild and dangerous spikes — which recalls us to the wilds Joseph Campbell was going on about in Arthurian legend. If you go into the desert early on in the game, or cross the wrong bridge and head into some

---

1. This is essential. Unlike contemporary capitalism, the game allows you to build savings and invest in your future. *Dragon Quest* games are many things, and one of them is generous. Imagine how much shittier the game would be if resting at an inn cost pretty much the exact same amount of gold you could get from depleting your hit points.

2. Getting defeated by monsters means you lose half your gold pieces. So essentially that werewolf mugged you, but left you with enough money to get back home. Again, a generous game.

3. You start the game with a stick. Straight up whaling on these monsters with the same tool any child has while wandering the forest and playing make-believe.

enchanted-ass woods, you will get right ruined by the werewolves and witches that haunt those haunts. So one "story" of the game, the story beneath the numerical scaffolding, is perseverance. The adventure is not knowing what places will destroy you and end your friction-y, grindy, treadmill of fun. The excitement comes from trying to figure out if you have enough metaphorical numbers to make it to the next stage of your journey.

Do you feel the math yet? It's all numbers. Some numbers jump out right into your face, like the hit points and the amount of "damage" that each swing of your sword does to a reanimated desert skeleton. Some numbers are metaphors for the simplistic growth that your avatar undergoes as he builds up the strength necessary to be a hero. (We could have a lot of fun unpacking all of the interesting facets nestled in that metaphor like a dragon in its cave, but I think I'll move on for now.)[1]

What's more, that numerical underpinning of the game was designed with such clean elegance that, when they re-released the game on the iPhone, and realized that people would be playing this on the toilet in five-minute bursts, they tossed a simple multiplier in there, across the board, and the entire game scaled along with it.

•

The other narrative scaffolding specific to video games is the atmosphere, which is best told through interaction. Films and books definitely have atmosphere, too, conveying a sense of place through the combined efforts of the artist's sensorial sketch and our imagination's love of filling in the blanks, but games do it a little differently.

---

1. The idea that anyone can win as long as they keep trying. The generosity of that spirit. The accessibility of that math to anyone who can input, how it doesn't depend on twitch reflexes unlike almost every other video game at that time.

In *Dragon Quest* games, that interactive atmosphere is told through the game loop of battles I mentioned above (which grant that spice of danger and adventuring into the unknown) contrasted against the city, settlements of peace in this world of chaos, filled to the brim with people. The vast majority of these people are, strictly speaking, irrelevant to the progress through the game. Only a few of them will have any information or quests that are key to defeating the Dark Lord. However, I would posit that the people are the point. Each one of them is sketched in a handful of lines of dialogue. Whenever you hit the context-sensitive action button, you talk to these folks. We never see what the protagonist says to start the conversation, a convention in games like this called the "silent protagonist," initially introduced because Yuji Horii never wanted a player to go, "Hey. I wouldn't say that!!"

So instead we have to fill in the blanks as our hero goes around chatting with all manner of townsfolk during their adventures. And these people, man, they are so well-rendered. Even though all we get is the tiniest vertical slice, it's like a keyhole window into a real life. Whatever their concerns or interests are, whatever they're caught up in, it helps paint the picture of this world.

The world of *Dragon Quest* is made up of people. That makes immanent sense in a game series devoted to saving the world. All of these little characters that you fall in love with as you zip around the world righting wrongs and overcoming monsters, that's who you're fighting for. Not some king. Not some legacy. Not because, abstractly, "it's the right thing to do." No, you are fighting for the individuals you meet who dish out their little, real lives, hopes, fears, failures, and successes, one line after another.

Each one[1] tells a little story, either in the single line, or over a few successive trips back to the city. Seasons change. Problems grow and go away. Concerns shift. These people make the world seem so much more real, emotionally, than I would have ever expected.

Interacting with these people is the true treasure of a *Dragon Quest* game. Gold and magic armour is just the fuel. Driving the car feels great, but it's all the stops along the way that make this journey so incredible.

Every single step is fun.

No wonder this game spawned a genre.

·

Given that foundation of math-feels and atmosphere, I want to talk about an Adventuring Dad of such visceral intensity that it could only exist within the framework of a *Dragon Quest*. His name is Pappas,[2] and he's from *Dragon Quest V*.[3] (If you don't want it spoiled, go download *DQV* onto your phone, play through the first three or four hours of the game, then come back. I'll be right here.)

Like all great fairy tales, *DQV* starts with a prophetic dream.

A king paces back and forth. His wife is in labour. The game is so fine-tuned to the theme of fatherhood that its opening seconds are about a man becoming a dad. There's trouble, it's a tricky childbirth. Omens flash.

Then you wake up. That king is your dad, Pappas, only now he looks rough. When you, a little kid, tell him about your

---

1. Okay, there are hundreds, maybe not each and every one, but pretty much.

2. In some translations it's "Pankraz," but screw that. He's Pappas.

3. Initially released on the Super Famicom (the Japanese version of the Super Nintendo) in 1992.

dream, he laughs it off and tells you to go get some fresh air. Turns out you and your dad are on a boat full of sailors. When you chat with these sailors, it becomes immediately apparent that your dad is *the shit*. Every single one of them respects your dad, thinks he's incredible, and some even owe him big time for favours in the past.

When you land on shore, your dad has some important business to talk about with the local official. Of course he does. Despite looking like a rough vagabond, almost everyone defers to your father. He's the man. So off you go, to poke around the docks, looking for something that might arouse a little kid's interest.

Quick break here to talk about immersion and storytelling. Despite being a cartoony fantasy fairy tale, this game is told with a tight third-person point of view. Every bit of information is coming through the filter of your little kid character. When he goes up to a signpost it says, "You can't read." Correspondingly, when you think about the way this kid interprets what people say about his father, that rock-star gleam that we universally receive *might* just be part and parcel of a child's admiration for their parent. Either that, or everyone you encounter in this world looks up to Pappas like he's their father.

Back to the game. Eventually you run out of things to check out on the dock and head out into the world, perhaps even by accident. Then we are right back into that fundamental *Dragon Quest* experience I noted above: wandering the world, hearing stirring adventure music, looking for the next stop in the horizon. Except this time you are a literal child. Not even a youth of destiny, but a preschooler. When you encounter the slimes that are the first monster you fight in every *Dragon Quest* game — they ruin you. Usually, slimes are a kind of nice throwback to the old games that the main character dispatches with aplomb, if not ease. But this time, in this one *Dragon Quest* game, no.

You are a child. Monsters are scary. Even grinning blue gum-
drop slimes.

It looks like you are going to fall, one step out on your
adventure.

Then Dad arrives. Out of nowhere Pappas swoops in.
Remember all those numbers that we talked about before,
carrying subliminal narrative weight? That skyrockets into a
whole new dimension. Because Pappas is impossibly powerful. He *destroys* those monsters with stupendous blows. His hit
point pool is enormous, dwarfing yours by several orders of
magnitude. He dispatches the monsters, heals his son's wounds,
and gives him a little lecture about wandering off on his own.
Then he escorts you from the port settlement to the first town
of the game, and each time you encounter monsters the result
is the same. Like any true father, Pappas protects you without
breaking a sweat.

The message is clear: Pappas is invincible. But this is where
it is important to recall the frame of this story: Pappas is invincible *in the eyes of his son*.

For the next few hours of the game, we get our feet wet
with little kid-sized adventures that happen on the margins
of a larger quest. We tag along after Pappas as he is trying to
figure something out. Or find something. We're never quite
sure because the grown-ups don't condescend to tell this little
kid what's going on. Instead, whenever the serious talk begins,
we're told to "go outside and play" and of course we find some
trouble, only now Pappas doesn't always bail us out. Within
the boundaries of these kidventures we must become somewhat
self-sufficient, even though, whenever we wander in the larger
world, Pappas is there to protect and guide us.

This eventually leads to a nearby king hiring Pappas to be
the bodyguard for his wayward prince, who just so happens to
be our age (and a pretty huge jerk). Even the king is somewhat

deferential to Pappas, thanking him for taking the time out of
his busy questing schedule to do the king a favour.

Then something from outside the frame shatters the status
quo. Hired goons kidnap the prince. Pappas tears after them.
We chase to try and catch up, but are of course not fast enough,
on our little kid legs. But we've learned how to endure, we've
discovered the grammar of adventure, and we press on to the
ruins where the kidnappers have taken the prince. Deep in the
dungeon, we find Pappas squaring off against some monsters.
It takes a lot of doing to get to him. When we do, he's surprised,
but, importantly, he doesn't chastise us like at the beginning of
the game. He realizes that we made it here by the dint of our
doughty arms, and he's impressed.

We rejoin our father in the corridors of this dank tomb,
ready to rescue the prince and get back on our own personal
quest. For one leg of the dungeon we get to roll with Pappas
one last time, and it is glorious. He is still a slaying machine.
Still head and shoulders and thick, muscly arms more powerful
than us, even after several hours of "levelling up." We do not
compare to our father. He is the man.

Then we meet the wizard who kidnapped the prince. He
sends his underlings after us. Pappas vanquishes them, because that's what Pappas does. Then the wizard grabs you,
the kid, and holds his wicked demon scythe to your throat.
And the game does something amazing. You go back into a
battle screen and are forced to watch the wizard's henchmen
beat Pappas to death. Bit by bit Pappas's incredible hit point
pool is chipped away, and he will not fight back, because he
cannot take the chance that the wizard will murder his
little boy.

Pappas stoically endures the assault. Each time it is his
"turn" in the battle, the game says, "Pappas takes a deep
breath." He doesn't know what to do. He is out of his league.

The wizard isn't playing by the rules. Your invincible father's prowess *doesn't matter* in the face of true evil. And you, as a child prisoner, are forced to watch this, beat after terrible beat.

This is an incredible inversion of the emotional stakes established by the game's previous structure. Whenever Pappas was in the party, we knew we were safe. We could relax. Dad could handle it; he could handle anything the world threw at us. In this terrible calamity, that illusion is sheared from our mind. We thought we were safe when Dad was around. Now we aren't. Now, we will never be safe again.

With his dying breath, Pappas says, "Your mother is still alive. Keep looking for her." Fade to black.

.

Ten long years pass by in that fade. You wake up a slave. The rest of the game sees you escape from a prison camp, carry on your father's quest, and become a father yourself. In fact, throughout the rest of the game, you are the shield that Pappas was for other people. For towns that can't fend for themselves, and for the eventual family that you build as you wander the world in search of answers.

Remember when I said every *Dragon Quest* game is about you saving the world from existential calamity? I lied. In *Dragon Quest V* you don't save the world. Your son does. You are a link in a chain and a shield for the true hero. You start off a little kid, but you must become a dad, attempting to live up to the impossible standards set by Pappas. Avenger of your father, saviour of your mother, and *not* the hero, but the hero's father.

The entire game is predicated on the prologue. Pappas's last words haunt *and drive* you throughout the entire game, as I'm sure they haunted the mind of the protagonist every single day he was shackled to the mad wizard's tower. The tiny slice of Pappas's life that we saw through the foggy glass of a child's perception acts as a foundation upon which we build ourselves and our life goals in earnest emulation.

Lastly, the game serves as a bit of everyday wisdom when it comes to a moment every son must one day face: the day he transcends his father's capacity. At the beginning of the game, Pappas's hit point total, that core number-metaphor that indicates just how heroic he is, is so high as to be unfathomable to our child selves. But, one day, if you keep grinding and growing, your own hit point pool will blast right past Pappas's. And you'll know full well that you aren't invincible, you aren't a paragon, you're just as confused and desperate as you were when you were a kid, trying to take the right step forward through a dark and merciless wood. You can suddenly stand shoulder to shoulder with the image of your father in your mind, and shatter the illusion.

Your dad was a scared, scarred man, wandering the world searching for his lost wife, trekking through the terrible wind of God, and doing his damnedest to shield you from it, until he couldn't.

•

It's disquieting, that moment, when you realize you are more of a "man"[1] than your father. That you might have been for some time now, if it weren't for the constant comparison to the invincible hero wrought from a child's horizons.

It happened to me quite late in life. A few years ago, my father and I were clearing some trees from a copse behind my grandmother's house. For a decade or so my dad and I had been going up to my grandparents' old farmstead to do all the chores that they couldn't. They piled tasks up all year long, like the

---

1. At least, in terms of stereotypical earmarks of masculinity: accomplishment, physical prowess, height, etc. Take your pick, they're all meaningless.

wood they used to heat their house instead of a furnace, the pile
getting higher and higher each year as old age, a bad heart, and
stomach cancer ate into my grandfather's physical capabilities.
I was lucky that I was working a seasonal gig that gave me the
summers off, because sometimes those work-vacations spanned
several weeks. I'd come back to Toronto tanned and, if not
ripped, at least a little thicker with labour-hewn muscles.[1]

Once my grandfather died, and my father retired, these
trips became his job. My life took a turn for the less-available,
and so my hands-on experience doing farm-y labour with my
dad dwindled. I'd go up when I could, and we'd work together,
but the dynamic shifted. More and more he was the foreman,
telling me what to do.

Then one fateful day, cutting down those cedar trees behind my grandmother's house, the image came asunder. We
had rigged up the trees with rope. The idea was to cut almost
all the way through them, then stand back and, from the opposite angle that the trees would fall, pull on them to snap the
last bit of the tree and be well out of the way. All it demanded
was a single strong pull. This was the kind of thing my dad was
always way, way better at than me. He has always been stronger
than me. He has a few inches and forty pounds on me. He is
not out of shape. But after chainsawing up at face-height and
working all day in the heat, and given the general toll of years,
when the time came to pull on that rope, he couldn't do it.
Then I did.

It was so weird, to be able to do something that he couldn't,
that it stuck with me all these years later as the moment when
that particular illusion dissipated. One I had been carrying my
entire life, seeing my dad as Pappas. Now I had as many hit
points as he did, or perhaps a few more.

---

1. My then-girlfriend, now-wife misses those returns.

•

Character growth in video games is generally predicated on power, and *Dragon Quest* is no different, but the incredible thing about *Dragon Quest V* is how it inverts the tropes that its previous iterations established as a means of telling a very effective and affecting story that, despite there being eleven sequels kicking around, *V* is still generally considered one of the, if not the, best *Dragon Quest* games.

As a central example of an Adventuring Dad bod, Pappas *and your character* undergo the outline of the narrative curve of a son growing into a father. This journey is punctuated with the friction of numbers and monsters, experience points and gold pieces, and the homespun wisdom of a modern fairy tale.

The violence, here, is a beat in that song. The friction comes from stopping throughout your wandering to test yourself against the growing strength of the monsters you encounter. That metaphor of progress defined against forward friction, and the hard numerical plateaus that accompany it, is shockingly similar to those moments in life when you realize — all of a sudden — that your whole world has changed, because some part of you did, without you realizing it. We can seldom see the experience points build up in real life, and even the level-ups tend to pass us by silently, making those few milestones we *can* see all the more precious and wonderful.

As a father, you get to see those milestones in your child. Because you've played this game before, you can anticipate the steps and stages in the text, even as the true player of the game is blissfully[1] unaware of the quantum leap ahead of them. So much has been said of the joy found in parenting when your child speaks their first word, or takes their first steps. Yet much

_____
1. And, in many cases, necessarily.

of that is predicated on the idea that it brings the magic of newness and wonder back into the parent's life. I wouldn't dare dispel that enchantment, but I would like to suggest that a big part of that vicarious wonder comes from the fact that we already know the rules of the game. That we have a correspondingly high level of frisson that comes from anticipating something that we know is coming, we just don't know when it will occur. So we build and childproof a space where a child can learn the manifold skills and abilities necessary to undertake the adventure of life.

We can appreciate a frame so much larger and scarier, beyond the comprehension of the child, and thus bear witness to our own power as we hold that world at bay and reinforce a garden wall for our children to grow up in through the sheer dint of our will. That joy is, in part, the joy in our own strength, and the knowledge we have that that strength is, in part, an illusion.

This take on parenting rather drips with emotion. It can infuse each day with meaning and wonder at our own capacities as parents, alongside our child's ever-burgeoning growth. They are interwoven joys, and I would never want to suggest that the one is legit and the other egotistical.

What's incredible about *Dragon Quest V*'s depiction of the relationship between Pappas and the protagonist is that it inverts the central emotional cue of the Adventuring Dad. Generally speaking, the wandering dad is one to whom emotion is, as with most traditionally male media, a problem to be overcome. The symbol of the child is one of the few rare outlets for emotional expression, and even then, especially in the old-school examples, it is a taut, tamped down, restricted emotional expression. A nod. A few words from an otherwise silent mien. A single, unseen tear blemishing a granite cheek as they pack their bags and move on to the next quest.

But not in *Dragon Quest V.* Here, the emotional drive is interwoven throughout the entire experience. Rather than use the child of the wanderer as an emotional release valve, the Adventuring Dad *dies* and is a fountain of grief and loss for the rest of the game as we try, forever, to live up to Pappas's image. Pappas's death isn't something that we sublimate, it's something we experience and carry with us. Emulating his example is not a dead act of mummery, but an attempt to breathe life into a dying world through the act of shepherding and nurturing others.

What's more, and this is really key, the protagonist in *Dragon Quest V* does not *and cannot* undertake this quest alone. You do it with a wife, and your children. You need all of them. You, the protagonist, might be a badass by the time you shrug off your slave collar and stomp out into the world in your imperial purple turban and ripped martial arts uniform — but you can't do the things your wife can do, and neither of you can do the things your kids can do. You're a complimentary team, which is so much more than a sum of its parts. You're a family.

•

Here, finally, we have an example of an adventurer that seeks integration, rather than a countercultural anti-hero who simply seeks annihilation and cathartic destruction. A wanderer who can stand for something, rather than merely stand in the way of something. Like, the Terminator is great, don't get me wrong. Love the guy. Great shades. But he had to die at the end of the movie. Not because of time paradoxes, but because he no longer served a purpose. It is impossible to imagine the Terminator, Sarah, and John enjoying a regular Sunday: pancakes at ten, catch a flick in the afternoon, maybe visit the in-laws for dinner (man, that'd be awkward). They can only exist within the confines of this conflict.

Or take a more recent example, also starring Viggo: *The Road*. A tender love story between a father and son wandering through a climate-change[1]-destroyed, postapocalyptic hellscape of cannibal clans and a completely unravelled society. In Cormac McCarthy's skeletal nightmare vision, one of the primary concerns for the father figure is that he does not actually stand for anything. He can merely sustain his son, a kind of miracle child because the boy still contains the impossible seed of goodness in this world with no future, no prospects, and, seemingly, no humanity. The interior landscape of the father is as barren as the world they trek through with their rickety shopping cart. Except for the love for his boy. The love that helps him do the impossible, and survive in a dead world. Classic Adventuring Dad stuff, the child being the only emotional outlet/purpose for a man forced to burden his way through existence.[2]

So once the child finds the future, a way out, a way forward, *another family* — dad has to go. Bye-bye, Viggo. Thanks for carrying me all those years.[3]

Not so in *Dragon Quest V*. Sure, one dad goes, but it's premature. It's a shock. Pappas is ripped out of your heart, a wound that never truly heals, a mirror you know you'll never fully reflect, let alone stand up to. But then you do. You have to. You've got no other choice. You become a father figure for your family, and your family a pillar of sanity in a world that's

---

1. Or whatever.

2. What a fun picture of fatherhood!

3. I admit: I'm being a bit flip to make the overarching point. On an emotional level, the idea of a father dying a little bit as their child approaches maturity is completely understandable. For a long, long time you sustain this little person-worm when they are so soft and defenceless. Every step they take toward adulthood means that the baby you fell in love with and gave your life for disappears, and the purpose with which you have galvanized all existence dies a little. Each step you celebrate with them is a step away from you.

lost its marbles. In *Dragon Quest V* we have a wanderer who stands *for* something while standing against everything, and as your family of adventurers ploughs through tides of monsters to the inevitable conclusion against the Dark Lord itself — you know it isn't toward an ending that they fight, but toward a beginning.

It's easy to imagine a life, and a purpose, for the hero beyond the frame of the text. That's an adventure worth fighting for.

The Wanderers Return

LET'S BE REAL: I WOULD be remiss if I didn't mention that the wandering-adventurer-badass-with-child was the germ of the entire dad bod concept. I am, if anything, a weird slurry of action movies and '90s-derived nerd culture.[1] Between 2018 and 2020[2] it seemed like there was a sudden resurgence of this particular bundle of dad tropes, with the wandering, reluctantly child-toting action heroes of *The Mandalorian*, *The Witcher*, and *God of War* all featuring a badass vagabond taking care of a kid. And they were huge multimedia blockbusters that shook mainstream culture in ways that I, living in my baby-driven exile,[3] was totally shocked to hear about. Heck, ladies in an

---

1. Which has, shockingly, become so successful commercially that it is now main-stream culture. I could not have imagined this at twelve. Like, I come from the gen-eration who carried shame like an obsidian albatross around my neck that I secretly loved *Dungeons & Dragons* hand-me-downs from my dad. When I talk to folks even a little younger than me, they love what they love and have no complicated relation-ship with it.

2. Both the time I became a father and the time when this book started to become a thing.

3. Not to mention my classic, knee-jerk artiste-wannabe disdain for any work that becomes too popular.

HR conference that I was facilitating were rapping large about the finale of *The Mandalorian*, when I hadn't even finished the first few episodes.

These three cyclopean dad bods of nerd culture, these three Adventuring Dads, are signs that one must beware. 'Ware the wanderers! They are canaries in the cultural coal mine, shrieking out tectonic demographic change.

•

Now that the groundwork has been laid for this wide-ranging dad bod archetype, I feel like I can wade into this pool of resurgent masculinity. Recall: the original wanderers were emotionally stunted individuals, the child performed the role of expressive catalyst, the wanderer had no partner, they stood apart from society in a mythical geography predicated on the interplay between order and chaos, and violence was the avenue to agency and successful masculine identity.

How do these new wandering, Adventuring Dad bods compare?

The Mandalorian is a *Star Wars* spinoff show that takes place after the fall of the Galactic Empire, repackaging the Wild West in space. It follows the adventures of a Mandalorian[1] bounty hunter named Din Djarin and his ward, Baby Yoda.[2] Like *Lone Wolf and Cub*, they are pursued by the politically powerful — remnants of the Empire who seek to control Baby Yoda's latent powers with the Force. The two wander the galaxy, take on bounty hunting jobs, and seek assistance in raising a young Jedi. Throughout, the gruff, always-helmeted Mandalorian learns to express care for Baby Yoda while balancing between chaos and

---

1. A cult of armoured bounty hunters first introduced in *The Empire Strikes Back* via Boba Fett, the guy with the helmet who captured Han Solo in a big ole slab of carbonite.

2. Yes, I *know* his name's really "Grogu," but in our hearts he'll always be Baby Yoda.

order: the strictures of Din's religion, the necessities of a dangerous and violent occupation, and the fractured, patchwork society of an empire in ruin.

The Witcher is a fantasy book series (by Polish writer Andrzej Sapkowski), video game trilogy, and television show set in an Eastern Europe–inspired continent populated by elves, wizards, and monsters galore. The series's titular protagonist is Geralt of Rivia, a witcher. Witchers are monster hunters trained from childhood, superpowered by mutation and magic. This mutation marks them as non-human,[1] so he's a de facto outcast from normal society. Initially, Geralt wanders from place to place, slaying monsters for cash, just doing his job. He embodies "the spirit of neo-liberal anti-politics"[2] that dominated Polish popular culture in the 1990s. He's a professional, staying out of the way of politics, which he sees as petty squabbling among decadent aristocrats. Then, somewhere along his journeys, he picks up Ciri, a young girl with tremendous latent powers, a troubled bloodline, and the heir to the throne of a recently conquered nation. Despite his frosty mutant demeanour, Geralt grows to love Ciri and raises her as his adopted daughter. This drags him into the cesspool of politics, as world powers seek to control Ciri's future.

The Mandalorian and *The Witcher* are basically two different shapes cut from the same cloth. Both are reluctant protectors of a child of destiny. Both are bounty hunters. Both perpetuate a nihilistic philosophy of quietude and non-intervention in some pretty obvious political and moral conflicts, choosing (at least

---

1. And makes witchers infertile, which means that they need to recruit children to beef up their ranks. As a collection of orphans and cast-offs, they don't really garner much respect.

2. From Péter Apor and Oksana Sarkisova, *Past for the Eyes: East European Representations of Communism in Cinema and Museums After 1989* (Budapest: Central European University Press, 2008), 198.

before their hearts are tugged awake by their ward) a strict diet of not getting involved. Heck, both even belong to a kind of martial cult during a time of political upheaval, with affiliation to neither the existing, waning power structure nor the rising one.

Instead, both are almost completely driven by individual connections predicated on personal histories and codes of honour, respect, and a somewhat amoral solitary ethos buttressed by the perceived needs of survival.

So they're both cowboys. I hope that's clear. A masked cowboy in space and a mutant cowboy with a silver sword. Classic adventure icons.

With *The Mandalorian*, that nostalgic trip is worn right on the protagonist's head, taking a bit villain from *The Empire Stikes Back* and turning him into an archetype for an entire culture: a minority space religion of orphans. Perfect. An entire community of children raised by adventurers become bounty hunters in a quest to armour themselves against the iniquities of life. I love it. That's some hype symbolism in a Disney+ space western where they literally call the protagonist a "gunslinger" in the press material.

Geralt of Rivia is, when you strip away the differences of setting, exactly the same guy: orphan, member of a bounty hunter warrior cult, shunned by society, armoured against emotional concourse (in this case magic and mutation expressed with his deadpan voice, shock of white hair, and yellow eyes as opposed to the more visual symbol of the Mandalorian's ubiquitous armour).

So of course these two lone wolves need a cub. Heck, Geralt's cool bounty hunter nickname is even "The White Wolf." Do these anti-heroes go on some wanton slaughter when bandits get in their way? Absolutely. Does their religion/job prohibit them from joining a community beyond their brotherhood? You bet. Do you only see them feel something for real when they lay their eyes on their destiny-laden charge? What do you think?

Their Adventuring Dad bona fides ring true like the hammer and tongs against the metal they both carry so ostentatiously, but what about innovations to the form?

As dad bods, these bounty hunters cleave so perfectly to the norm that it is honestly remarkable.

The biggest deviation for *The Mandalorian* is the construction of a found family around the protagonist and his ward. The inclusion of other misfits from within and without the Mandalorian's sect runs counter to the lone-wolf set-up and broadens the emotional web through which the Adventuring Dad wanders. By having others who act as a family, similar to *Dragon Quest V*, there is continuity of accountability, and conflict that needs to be resolved through means other than laser blasting.

The next innovation is that the Mandalorian is allowed emotional expression. It is subtle, given the non-stop helmet, but it is real. There are tender moments between the bounty hunter and Baby Yoda, up to and including cuddling on the spaceship as they hurtle through the cold void together.

When it comes to *The Witcher*, things are a bit more complicated. Book, game, and show portray different time slices of the same narrative scaffolding. A bunch of the crazy-successful[1] 2015 video game *The Witcher 3: The Wild Hunt* takes place way, way after the Adventuring Dad section of Geralt's life. In it, Ciri is grown up, confronting her siren call with duty and destiny, and you are playing catch-up along her trail, trying to piece together what, if anything, you can still offer in the form of protection and guidance. Given that you spent ten

---

1. As in, sold-fifty-million-copies successful. That's more than twice as many as the book series, which "only" sold fifteen million copies worldwide.

years teaching this orphan[1] the ways of the witcher cult (without, it should be noted, indoctrinating her into its drug rituals) the idea that she might still need your protection is a bit of a patronizing lede. And you know what? The game doesn't shy away from discussing that. In one of the key dramatic decisions you can make, one that determines which version of the ending you see in this one-hundred-plus-hours-long tromp through a monster-infected world,[2] is whether or not you are dad enough to admit that your ward no longer needs your protection. That she can handle herself in the cosmic war to come, given that she's the child of destiny and all that.

So too Mando, but in a different way. After acceding to the need for family, the old helmet recognized that he needed to give up sole proprietorship so that his little Jedi could learn how to protect himself from the big, dark galaxy. So they seek Jedi to help raise Baby Yoda, and eventually are rescued by the greatest lightsaber wielder of all time, Luke Skywalker.[3]

Unlike the roots of the Adventuring Dad archetype that sees death as the only reasonable response to your child/ward growing up, these two new Adventuring Dads derive meaning from other parts of life, and are interested in teaching their cubs something beyond slaughter — maybe not the good life, but at least a life ethic. Sure, it's generally contained within the parameters of a job, or some kind of job-cult, but it is a hell of a lot more than thumbs-upping from a vat of molten steel, or forever rolling your baby cart from one ninja ambush to another.[4]

---

1. Always orphans, those seeds of destiny.

2. Where, in classic *Twilight Zone* fashion, the real monster is man, am I right?

3. Of course, *The Book of Boba Fett* messes this ending up, but the crux is that in the critical moment Mando was able to recognize the need for Baby Yoda to join a greater community than their dyad.

4. Even worse, Ogami Ittō perishes in a duel with his nemesis that ran 178 pages in the original *Lone Wolf and Cub* manga. What a way to go.

These new Adventuring Dads can imagine a future. For their surrogate children and, more importantly, for themselves. Together. That gives them a reason to fight, sure, but it also gives them a reason to do something so much more important. Build.

They can do so because their backstory includes community. Outcast, minority communities that look after their own and carve out a life in ... not quite opposition so much as tension with the mainstream society they are one thread of. Both the Mandalorian and the Witcher are also provided the incredible leeway of being violent male characters who have and express emotions. They care about their wards, and unlike the robots and samurai of old they can show that directly. Sure they're rusty at it, given that the majority of their social interactions occur in taverns in the countdown to one brawl or another, but Din Djarin and Geralt of Rivia both learn how to be foster dads by accepting this limitation and learning from their mistakes. Throughout their stories they grow more tender, more expressive, all without losing the killer's edge.

These two Adventuring Dad bods nudge the archetype forward, one quest at a time.

*

God of War (2018), on the other hand, known across the internet as "Dad of War," is another kettle of tropes entirely. Slippery ones. Metafictional ones.

The premise of the game is brilliant. Take a bog-standard blockbuster game genre, the over-the-shoulder action game, and add a totally cinematic artistic limitation: it must be "filmed" all in one continuous shot. When I first heard that's what they were doing, I thought about *Russian Ark*, a feature-length experimental movie filmed in one take that escorts the viewer through a re-enacted history of the Winter Palace in Saint Petersburg. *Russian Ark* weaves together Russian history and art history in a single shot that features a cast of over two thousand extras performing a big ole soiree as they dance in a full Victorian ball. It is an incredible feat, logistically, and any time I tried to show someone that movie back in film school they'd fall asleep.

With a video game, or any animation for that matter, the logistics aren't even a thing. You don't need some Hercules of a camera op to make a full production in one shot. Instead, you need a creative vision in order to upend the visual grammar of cinema that depends on the cut as part of its core production of meaning, pacing, interest, sympathy, interrelations between characters, and establishment of the mimetic space. Editing is king. To take away that core feature seemed nuts, and like it would transform the game into a kind of aesthetic of endurance. Not a slog, necessarily, but a narrative space where the player would be hungry for a break, desperate for a chance to step away from the bold witnessing intrinsic to the no-blink single shot. A deep need for some way to release that constant, low-tension buildup.

Oh, right, it's a video game. You get that every time you hit a button. The game's excellent play-friction and game loop meant that there was a cycle of emotional engagement, a sine wave of witnessing and violent expulsion of tension with each dip into an in-game cinematic and each step forward along the hero and son's brutal, troll-strewn path.

Once I figured that out, it sounded structurally genius.

The main guy behind *God of War* was Cory Barlog, the game's director and co-writer. His story intersects with the story I'm trying to explore as I unravel the chains of meaning wrapped around this weird, yet entirely normal, Adventuring Dad bod game.

You see, *God of War* (2018) is a reboot of sorts. There were three other mainline *God of War* games before this one, so removing the roman numeral in 2018 highlighted a thematic reboot despite the fact that the game continues the story after the plot of the first three games. They officially called it a "re-imagining." A what? Okay, bear with me. Let's lay it out.

The first three *God of War* games were, like, shitty rock and roll. Cock rock. Big muscles. Weird, inappropriate tribal tattoos. Naked chicks for no reason. The protagonist, Kratos, rolls around mythological Greece killing everyone. Kill kill kill. Power is the name of the game. Power and prestige. You are the god of war and you have to prove that over and over again in the most individualistic one-man-war-against-ole-Zeus kind of way. Kratos kills everyone barring his path, first to become the god of war, then because he wants to upend the gods' authority. Kratos's weapon of choice is two massive axe-knives with a chain between them. Did I call it cock rock? Let's say hair metal instead. Goblin metal? I don't know.

Regardless, these games were released from 2005 to 2010, when the main cohort of male game-likers were in their teens and twenties, brains still dripping with adolescent chemicals, and the entire medium was predicated on leveraging and pumping exactly this kind of sauce for massive, massive male power fantasy profit.

Cory Barlog worked on those earlier games as lead animator, story writer, and game director. Then he quit that studio. Then he came back. For this one job. Like *Commando*.[1]

In this game, Kratos is done with mythical Greece and has moved up north to the mythical Norse land of Midgard. He has a wife, Faye, and a son, Atreus. They live a simple life in the woods, subsistence farming and hunting, far removed from the protagonist's pantheon-slaying past. Before the game starts,

---

1. Or *Unforgiven*, Clint Eastwood's incredible revisionist western about a Dad Going on an Adventure *one last time*.

Faye dies, and her last wish is to have her ashes scattered over the highest peak in the realm.

So we've got our quest, our impetus to wander, and our boy. Kratos literally calls him "boy" throughout the entire game.[1] We've also got reason to slay: the gods and monsters of this land don't take kindly to Kratos and his quest. Why? Turf wars, basically.

As a dad, it is immediately apparent that Kratos dances to a traditional drummer. He is a very strict disciplinarian, both explicitly and implicitly leveraging the concept of capital-D discipline as a core value. He's also, what we call in the business coaching and consulting world, "acting from the unilateral control mindset."[2] He withholds information. He commands. He is super strict without any explanation about why these rules make sense, as though they are just given. And, again, like many Adventuring Dads before him, Kratos the emotional control freak has the excellent justification of the environment. Everywhere this father and son turn, something malefic is trying to stomp them to death, or rend their deific flesh.

The twist is that, well, the kid probably *should* figure out a reasonably high-performing level of emotional control because, as a godling, he has massive latent powers and — like the depictions of gods in so many cultures — would become an insufferable dick without a strict code of conduct and the reins of a healthy superego.

Violence and Emotional Control Coach aside, *God of War* has two other facets worthy of investigation. Unlike *Dragon Quest V* or the two neo-cowboys above, it has no reason to

---

1. "Good shot, boy." "Keep your expectations low, boy, and you'll never be disappointed." "I'm a god, boy."

2. An egocentric, fear-driven, zero-sum approach to teamwork. As opposed to the "collaborative mindset" exemplified by transparent communication, humility, curiosity, and compassion.

build, except for the relationship between father and son. A big part of why Kratos wants to try to teach his son, Atreus, self-control is that he doesn't want his son to follow in his footsteps. When Kratos was younger, he was a rageaholic who murdered his own father on one of his many kill-benders. He wants Atreus to learn anger management, stop the generations-long blood feud between progeny and progenitor,[1] and break that chain of violence. The problem is that what he's offering isn't much better: it's a different kind of chain, one of strict control and a silent and cold lack of tenderness.

When Atreus flips out later in the game, revealing the extent of his own powerful rage, not only do I really begin to see the point behind Kratos's parenting style, but I see the recognition of self on Kratos's face. He knows he's seeing a version of himself, falling for the same traps he did, because of the same flaws that poison his own heart.

That is the face of real dadship.

I tasted the tiniest sip of that drink one night, when my son and I were sitting around the dinner table alone. My wife had left the table to be in a meeting, and L— and I were hanging out as we often do at the tail end of meals. These days, he takes a long-ass time to clear his plate, but he really doesn't want to leave until he's taken care of every crumb. So we sit in affable silence, or we chat about his day at preschool, as I cajole slow bites into his maw.

On the night in question, L— and I were both wearing button-up flannel shirts. Flannel shirts are a thing in the Cruise pantheon. My dad wears them a lot. I wear them to the point of it being a character trait. At L—'s baby shower, we received a lot of baby flannel shirts, so that he'd fit in.

---

1. Which is a totally normal result of a hereditary monarchy with immortal rulers, now that I think about it.

After a bite of zucchini, my son smiled and looked at me with a twinkle in his eye. He pointed at my chest, then at his. He said, "Daddy and me. Both wearing buttons!" Then he counted the little black buttons down his torso.

"That's true," I said warmly. "We're both wearing button-up flannel shirts."

Then he looked at me. I've never seen that look before or since. It was electric, pure recognition and satisfaction. He saw that he was the same as his father. My son saw me[1] as an image to emulate, and he approved. He was happy, perhaps proud, of the similarity between us.

The fear flashed through my bowels.

I know I'm not worthy of emulation. I'm a sack of misshapen flaws parading as a person. What if he picks up my crippling indecision? What if he inadvertently mimes my grotesque inability to listen, or my slithering cowardliness when it comes to saying what people want to hear? What if he sees through to the essential weakness at my core?

None of this showed on my face, because I was simultaneously bathed in pure, radiant pride. My son looked up to me as a figure worthy of emulation. Nothing could so bolster my self-esteem. I could do anything, I could be anything, fuelled by that glimpse from my boy.

These twinned opposites coil and writhe, chewing on each other's tails.

I so desperately want to be what my son sees in me, as often as I can, and, simultaneously, help him accept the flaws he finds in his own soul (inherited or otherwise) so that he can transcend the flickering shadows his father never could.

I can imagine Kratos feeling the same, and Cory Barlog for that matter.

---

1. *Me?!*

Early on in the game, Kratos chastises Atreus for assuming that Kratos's silent mourning is less authentic than Atreus's totally normal outbursts of grief. And, sure, that's legit. Your feels are just as real, no matter how (or if) you express them. But if you are trying to help someone break the cycle of *your own behaviour* and learn from the mistakes of the past, a very important step forward is to incorporate a healthy relationship with your internal landscape, rather than feeling like it is absolutely essential to never allow any humanity to seep through the cracks of your emotional armour.

I don't know about you, but when I was a young male person, raised by our culture to have a certain kind of incongruent relationship with emotions (namely, don't have any, and if you do, keep them to yourself),[1] that taught me to project that incongruency onto others, and onto any emotional expression that I stumbled into. And it really *felt* like stumbling into them, despite the fact that they were obviously building within the other person just like they build in me (or anybody) but I was so trained, again and again, to delete the possibility of emotional congress and expression, of empathetic listening, from my conceptual vocabulary that when, say, a partner who was upset would burst into tears, I would be kind of shocked and disturbed. It was very gross. I would treat the emotional expression the same way as someone walking into a room with dog shit on their shoes. Like, "Eww, get that out of here."

At different stages of my development, I might have tried to talk them out of their emotions. Get to the root of it using the Socratic method, show them that the intense expression they

---

1. I should say, not from my parents. They did a great job of providing latitude for my super-sensitive self. But in the world, sensitive males are not exactly rewarded for this behaviour.

were manifesting all over my carpet wasn't logically sensible, rush through all kinds of reasons and rationales for why the malefactor, or situation, or whatever they were encountering — why it might have happened, as though *explaining it away* did a damn thing.

At others, I would try to hold them, but my body was so stiff, my response so wooden, that it was equally weird and gross. My entire body language radiating waves of discomfort and revulsion at the bare fact that these emotions were happening.

I couldn't sit with that discomfort. I couldn't listen without opening my big mouth. I couldn't be there for other people. Deep down, I knew that this was not the way. But I had no other.

Neither does Kratos. His warrior ethos does not allow for comfort. He's a man of action. Sensitive, empathetic listening is not perceived as an activity.

The crazy thing is, all evidence indicates Cory Barlog *does* get it and tries to model this behaviour. It's hard to say. And here is where this essay gets metafictional.

·

The day *God of War* was released, Cory Barlog[1] published a video on his personal YouTube channel. It was, and is, the only video on his YouTube channel. It's five minutes long. It is everything. This entire book, the entire conceit of dad bod, is in this video. I think. Maybe. I'm going to try my best, here, to translate some of that energy. I know I will fail, before I've even started, but I have to try. For me. For my son. For Cory, and his.

The video is titled "God of War Review Reaction Video from Director Cory Barlog," which is as prosaic as it is SEO-savvy. Cory sits in front of his webcam, in a poorly lit bedroom,

---

1. I keep typing "Balrog."

about to open up the Metacritic page for the game. Metacritic is an aggregate of video game reviews from reputable news outlets. Game reviews come out all at once on release day. *God of War* had a lot of budget, a lot of attention, and, as an exclusive release for Sony, a corresponding lot of pressure.

In the days of pre-Covid, a video like this was pretty intimate. We're looking into this guy's house. He's poorly lit. It's grainy footage. He's wearing regular clothes. Despite being the director of a game with a budget the size of two or three Hollywood movies,[1] Cory radiates tension and hesitation.

He then explains what we're all doing here. He's procrastinating. He's waiting to see the reviews, but he is also terrified that the game will be an international flop. All it would take is the red pen from fifty or so video game journalists at select outlets around the world, and five years of this guy's life would be down the toilet.

Deep breath. He clicks the link. Instant relief, followed by shimmering emotions across his face. He breaks down and cries on camera. He discusses how he just didn't know if this would work, if a game like this would connect with people, if he was crazy. Then, appropriately, he pivots to talk about all of the other people, all of the work that went into crafting a game like this. Thanking them all for their hard work.

And the tears continue. "I didn't fuck it up," he says, voice catching throughout this incredibly weird vlog. He is vulnerable. He is openly crying. He is awkward.[2] Disbelieving. Uncertain. Self-aware and self-effacing. Cory Barlog is human. Too, too human in this five-minute video of a man seeing what other people think about the art he helmed. He is everything

---

1. At least.

2. So awkward, I have a very hard time listening to my cynical self who says, "Ah, the whole thing is a PR stunt."

Kratos isn't, and could never be, in his thirty-hour romp around Midgard. And, even though it seems as though, at least in part, Barlog is doing this for himself, making a display for the press of the game, it turns out that he is doing this for an entirely different reason than I had initially anticipated.

Here's the description of the video:

> *First, sorry about the quality. Shot on my macbook webcam. So, I thought a lot about whether or not to upload but then I thought about what my son, Helo, is going through right now. He doesn't want us around when he is sad, opting to run in another room and yell at us if we try to come in. It has been important to us to let him know that it is OK to be sad, it is OK to cry. There is nothing to hide. I thought I would try to set a good example and show him that papa can cry in front of the world, or at least the 50 people who end up watching this. :) This is for you, Helo. Papa loves you.*

As of writing, the video has over two million views. Top comments[1] range from supportive to disbelieving that someone with the talent to direct and write a game like this could be so full of doubt. Unlike the vast majority of video-game-focused YouTube content, in these comments, people are being human toward another person. Doing all the things that Adventuring Dads can't do, because we live in a world where we don't have to kill to survive, and empathy is a far more powerful tool than a gun.

•

I don't even care if it was a PR stunt. I don't care that it is kind of weird to put a video like that out into the world for your kid. It is modelling a new masculinity, one predicated on a wider

---

1. Never read the comments!

definition of what it means to be a man than we were given. Of course it's going to have stumbles, or be interwoven in weird egotistical devices. We're discussing pop culture, after all. Part of the point is that people need to pay attention to the thing for it to justify its existence.

Barlog cares about his son enough to put himself out there in a way that is unabashedly not cool. Even if you find it admirable in intent, you are still being asked to sit down with someone as they go through something. It is uncomfortable. Ten years ago, I would have had a cognitive kill switch flip in my head, writing the whole video off as inauthentic due to the sheer fact that it was shared on social media. Now, I don't know. Like so much of this trail of analysis, I find myself ending on a conundrum.

And look, pot vs. kettle, here. The performativity of being a good dad, or trying to be, or not knowing how to be — I'm literally sitting right here writing a book about those very concerns. Just because I'm hiding behind an analysis of stories and shows, let's be real: I'm talking about myself here. I'm crying all over every page. For me to question the authenticity of Barlog because of his five minutes of doubt in front of a webcam would be arch hypocrisy.

This is definitely progress, of a sort. But not in the text itself. Without that metafictional layer of Barlog's vlog, the dad bod of *God of War* would be incredibly incomplete, a mere shadow of the possibility space that emerges with that additional five minutes of human frailty.

It would be, like *The Mandalorian* and *The Witcher*, like *Dragon Quest V*, a half-step in the right direction. A dad bod worth dissecting, but still not one to emulate, given the overwhelming constraints of the genre's addiction to violence.

Wait. Is that what I'm looking for? A fictional character to emulate? To base my new identity on?

It sure seems like I desperately want a new way of being a man to emerge, and yet I keep looking for it in this totally inappropriate cauldron of commercial art. Hints and mirages do twinkle at the edge of my vision, but is this entire project doomed to find mere sketches and outlines?

What more could I expect, really?

Wouldn't that be okay, if there was no version worthy of emulation? Calling all the way back to Old Joe Campbell up above, looking for an authority, a dad bod to call my own, a way set down in stone that I could follow — that's not the way things are heading anymore, man. We have to choose for ourselves. We have to craft an entire value system out of the dust and the blood of our forebears. Not just the dads and the men in the room, obviously; think about all of the folks who live in ways unsanctioned by mainstream society — you think they're waiting around for a model? Sure, representation is nice, and actually super helpful, but that doesn't mean that people are trying to *be* those representations. Even the super meaningful ones are but two-dimensional images that must be fleshed out in our own lives due to the fact that real life has so many more variables than any form of art. By necessity, art is choosing what to leave out from life.

But I was raised an able-bodied white guy, and when I was a kid, the way most stories were still told about and to guys just like me, it almost felt sensible to think that there was a model out there, of a man, of a dad, of a person, that I could just crib and be fine.

It sounds nuts when I lay it out like that, but the deeper I go in my dissection of dad bods, the more I can feel that desperation, that hunger, climbing up alongside the bile in my bowels.

The weakest parts of me want someone, anyone, to tell me how to be a dad. Our society, these shards of culture, or that glimmering look I received from my boy.

Like Viggo at the end of *A History of Violence* I'm sitting there, with an empty plate, waiting for my son to spoon over some sustenance. That's not fair. It's my job, not his, to provide.

And yet he does.

Over and over again.

INTERLUDE:
Gandalf vs. Obi-Wan

Dads of Destiny

WHO IS A BETTER DAD, Gandalf or Obi-Wan Kenobi? These are two titanic dad bods of contemporary cinema and speculative fiction, from the cousin genres of fantasy and science fiction,[1] who North American filmgoers and meme-makers have latched onto with fierce paternal affection.

In the sci-fi corner: everyone's favourite man of failed prophecies and regretful hermitage, the character that introduced the world to the Force and my generation to the idea of a main character dying in the first episode — Obi-Wan "Old Ben" Kenobi.

In the fantasy corner: you know him, you love him, he loves you, and he is *not* some conjurer of cheap tricks — Gandalf the Grey, a.k.a. Gandalf Stormcrow, a.k.a. the Grey Pilgrim, or as the elves know him, Mithrandir.

At their core, they are the same Zen-dad archetype.

Both educate by misdirection, both of them have personal power levels and powerful networks that they eschew in favour

---

1. Although, given laser swords and the Force, I'd be hard-pressed not categorizing *Star Wars* as "Science Fantasy," but that feels a bit too pedantic even for me.

of a mundane existence of fireworks and dry country living (i.e., they both like to drink beers on the weekend rather than play power broker with the political or economic elite), and the thing that truly binds them together is that they both play the same narrative function: accepting the orphan as a potential hero.

At first glance, this feels like a kind of base criteria for some real hero-level dadliness: if you can't accept an orphan who is not your real kid, then you are on some baby-level dadship. Any dad of salt and merit wants to believe that he, too, is the kind of man who could accept an orphan into his heart.

Importantly, neither of these orphans are *just* orphans. They are heroes, because that is what a story demands. Especially these Campbellian Hero's Journey–type stories, which present an extra criterion for champion-level dadliness presented through this dad bod that, actually, weakens and dilutes the example of these two wizards: the *actual* orphans are left out in the cold. They don't serve a purpose unless they're heroes, and if they're heroes then they are serving *your* purpose, you manipulative wizard!

The scales of dadliness become twisted when there is this exchange between dad and orphan, this investment. Can we truly trust or applaud a father figure who is in it to win it? Who is in it, it seems, for themselves? For glory and winning a war?

To transport these themes into the real world, what about *actual* orphans? Is the value of this form of fatherhood, as we might imagine it, judged on a sliding scale of how much presumed disaffection you can conquer? The more tragic the orphan's story, the more justified the love? Eww. As though love needs justification. And again, as with the adventurers and the cowboys and Rambo's demon dads, paternal affection is translated into muscular terms of emotional Return on Investment and the utility of orphan-heroes to save us in our old age like a living piggy bank or a security against the indifference of our biological (or non-existent) children.

It all comes back to heroes, again. And sure, we want to view the orphans in our lives (whether they are actual orphans or social ones) in heroic terms, because they are *within the frame of their lives*, but that's totally different from the global use these Zen-wizards put these kids through. What these movies expose is that this vision of foster fatherhood is ultimately hollow and unrealistic *every time you expect an orphan you save to become a hero*.

Can adventure fiction uncouple this characterization from the demands of plot? Can we show orphans that they are heroes, without asking them to, one day, save us?

Or the inverse: the true measure of a father is someone who raises a child, any child, to become a hero that saves someone else. But not you. Never you.

.

What twists the question further is that Gandalf and Obi-Wan are also dads of something more than a character, they are dads of destiny, because each carries the fate of their respective cosmos on their bearded shoulders.[1]

Within the boundary of the main tale, their stories hit the same beats: they find a nobody, raise them up, take them on an incredible journey beyond the borders of their small, provincial life; give them the tools to grow beyond their own limitations and perceptions and deal with the physical dangers of this new, conflict-ridden sphere; then they peace out, folding

---

1. Other examples include the obvious Dumbledore, who feels a bit like a Zellers-level Gandalf, depending on what decade you were born in, but I'm old so I'm sticking with the originals and not the photocopy. Or Morpheus from *The Matrix*. They're all wizard-Zen-dads with access to spooky knowledge and initiation into a world of adventure.

in on a flaming red sword from a dark, mysterious villain who is way, *way* too powerful for our protagonists to handle; they fall into darkness, only to be reborn as a guiding force of pure, shimmering light, their beard newly manicured, their robes bleached, their purpose unabated.

Gandalf is more of a Bodhisattva; he can't help but keep his finger in the pie on the physical plane even though he refuses to act directly except in cases of the most extreme duress. Why? Why not lend an eagle to our furry-footed Ring-bearer?

Obi-Wan is more of a spiritual father, helping our star orphan initiate his journey into the unseen realm, which will equip him with the necessary space-wizard fortitude to assert balance in a complicated, generations-long religious blood feud.

Gandalf is not interested in balance. War in Middle-earth is much more genocidal and drawn on ethnic lines. Again, Gandalf is neither an ethical nor a spiritual guide, but more a pragmatic and psychological one, much like the core Mahayana texts. He does as much as he can without unleashing his big-time magic because, I assume, doing so will attract the vengeful fire-eye of Sauron, the evil ... sentient tower? Like: I always think of that scene in *The Hobbit* when Gandalf dispatches the pack of wargs by hotting up some pinecones until they become ember grenades and tossing them at the wolves' tails. This is a dude who can go toe to toe in a mile-long descent into underdarkness against a winged[1] demonspawn with the light of elder gods on his side, and he's playing s'mores with some dogs rather than shattering their bones. I assume he's got reasons, but Gandalf ain't sharing. He is very big on a regimen of Need to Know.

---

1. How can I write this word so you know I'm saying "wing-ed" like a British instructor?

Obi-Wan, on the other hand, is super hands-off. Once he rips Luke out of his comfort zone, chops off a bar patron's arm, hypnotizes a few state troopers, and they get into space, he basically gives the boy a few catchphrases and makes a beeline for his own demons.[1] He passes off the real training regimen to Yoda and takes on more of a cosmic consulting role as far as the central conflict is concerned, phoning in to catch up with Luke and offer him pointers along the way. Even though this feels a bit like copping out, at least in the parenting department, it actually highlights Obi-Wan's commitment to helping Luke grow beyond a dependency.

Let's be honest, the homespun heroes of *The Lord of the Rings* would fall flat on their faces if it wasn't for Gandalf thumbing the scales every chance he gets. Frodo can only handle facing off against an *artifact* of Sauron's, not an agent, and certainly not the Big Bad himself. Even in his first movie, Luke doesn't sneak onto the Death Star and drop a grenade into the lava core of the station — the kid basically drives a motorcycle with wings into Fort Knox and snipes the self-destruct switch with a Nerf gun. Then, with just a bit of training, he *goes after* Darth Vader, and pays with his hand. That's some iterative learning! That's training your grit! Talk about growth mindset.

Frodo, on the other hand, succumbs to the ring in the end (although I guess you could say Luke succumbs to his anger and the Dark Side, at least momentarily, a synecdoche for the kind of power hunger interwoven in the One Ring's modus operandi) and if it wasn't for Gollum, why, Middle-earth'd be in a bad place. Heck, even Frodo's loss pales in comparison to Luke's: Frodo loses a finger, Luke loses a hand, loses his image of his own father — taking the last step in his disillusion

---

1. A.k.a. Darth Vader, Obi-Wan's initial, stupendous failure as a surrogate father figure.

— *and* takes the first step in replicating his father's descent
into Nietzschean inhumanity. Then Luke gets an entire other
movie to one-up his mistakes and transcend them in the tangible world, unlike old bow-out-of-the-action Kenobi. Luke
acts both spiritually and emotionally, in the real world, against
not only the dark demon of Darth but also the demon's puppet
master — who I guess is Sauron-level (except, now that I think
about it, a successful Sauron) — a.k.a. the Emperor.

But Luke is a sky prince. Frodo has no inherited ability to
manipulate the underlying energy of the cosmos. Maybe Obi-
Wan had nothing to do with it? That's a fair cop. Judging a
father based on the fruits of his loom is a sick shell game.

And, for what it's worth, even though Gandalf came back
to lead armies and whisper secrets into some king's cobwebbed
ears and dunk on his old boss by redirecting a river into his
office — he did let Frodo go. No, wait, that was Aragorn. Was
Aragorn operating as an agent of Gandalf's intent? It's a messy
operation.

The main thing is that Gandalf is playing interference,
glowing white hot to distract the flaming eye from the two
wee nobodies creeping through the cryptic swamps of Mordor.

Which one is a better dad? What are my criteria here?
Stepping back: Who fathers fate better, who better bears fate
on their shoulders, who better dads destiny? Or maybe just:
Stepping back to our hot take on orphan manipulation above,
are they both merely exploiters? Placing a higher calling above
the protagonist they are basically sacrificing to the needs of
the cosmic conflict? I mean, both protagonists come out …
irrevocably changed.

And yet they seem to truly care for their charges. They are
juiced-up versions of the Adventuring Dad bod, in part because
of their beards and cosmic knowledge, but also because of the
concentrated need and attention placed upon their wards. Both

Geralt the witcher and the Mandalorian would like us to think that they, too, are shepherding a scion, but, importantly, *they are the stars of the show.* Not Ciri. Not Baby Yoda. That structurally supportive role in the narrative matrix places Gandalf and Obi-Wan into a different category of dad bod, one that hits a much more primary dadliness vibe, like the ultimate Adventuring Dad, Pappas, in *Dragon Quest V.*

It sucks, but at a certain time in your kid's life you are better off Obi-Wanning it and fading into the universal cosmic noise rather than demanding folks look to the east as you ride in on the last lord of the horses. That steals your kid's thunder, and it manifests in countless permutations in this far, far away galaxy of ours. It's hard to step away, to let them hurt themselves, and learn hard truths on their own. But do you really think Luke would've been able to get his shit together if right off the bat, when Luke was still wet with sand behind his ears, Obi-Wan had been like, "Yeah, your dad was literally the strongest Jedi. I chopped his arms off once, didn't even slow him down. Plus also he performed a few religious/ethnic cleansings, on both sides of a war, and nowadays is the COO of the Galactic Empire." Luke's stoke would've totally died. There was no way to see the through-line to Jedi Knight from that dry puddle of a planet, and Obi-Wan had the wisdom to lie.

That's what shouldering fate takes. Hard truths for a harder time.

Gandalf, on the other hand, doesn't bother shielding the hobbits from the scope of the world's calamity because he assumes their role in it will be minimal. Carry this piece of jewellery to Elrond's estate, then let the heavy lifters do the real work. Gandalf is the hockey dad who wants to leap off the bleachers and strap on the skates to show those peewees how it's really done. The kind of dad who never "takes it easy" on his kids, because how'll they learn how to compete in the real world unless they are crushed by someone they could never conceivably compete with over and over again? (That's what it would've been like if Obi-Wan had told Luke the truth right off the bat. Spiritually crushed like a seven-year-old arm-wrestling a Joe Six-pack dad.) Heck, even Darth Vader isn't that cold. Darth takes it relatively easy on Luke the first few times they tangle, because he's got a sense of fair play and an eye on the long game. It's only when the B-list hobbits show their mettle with guerilla eco-terrorism that Gandalf starts to (reluctantly) share quest privileges with them.

Gandalf can only retreat from the world when the quest is done.

Obi-Wan knows that if you want to activate your kid, you've gotta bow out as soon as the quest takes shape. Then nudge, a little, but only when they really need it.

Do their approaches/results differ so much because of the different goals that they have, the circumstances that they're in, or the philosophical differences between Zen-wizard-dads in the 1950s vs. the 1970s? Eradication vs. Balance, Leading vs. Enabling, the qualities of your vessel of fate vs. the qualities of your allies ...

By all accounts, Obi-Wan should be way more desperate, and yet he's the one willing to lie back in the cut and watch things play out with minimal supervision.

To take another tack, how do I want to look at my son? It doesn't seem super healthy to place him in so central a universal core as Luke, or a traumatized Frodo who seeks therapy in an elven institution across the sea. If that's your measure of a dad, both Zen-wizards fail.

I think I'd prefer some of the more noble goals of Merry and Pippin, who focus their attention on the local community by becoming mayors or something of the Shire. Gandalf's boy band brood is always waiting for him to save the day; that dependency is no good. Obi-Wan's style of nudge and phrasing at key moments seems really appealing, but not quite enough and not quite the right perspective in terms of the personhood of the child. I don't want my son to put that much pressure on himself, especially if he sees me as folding too much into my own robes.

It's tricky to draw these dads of destiny back out into the real world, in part because they are so far removed, but in part because applying their stakes to fatherhood isn't helpful when you aren't in a war,[1] star or otherwise.

I'm not trying to redress a religious schism with political consequences, nor am I trying to eradicate an ancient foe. I'm trying to build toward a better future, which is something neither Gandalf nor Obi-Wan can supply. They come from different eras, lost to time, which is why they are either wanderers, hermits, or recluses who fade away when the action is done. They serve no purpose in the rebuild. And, sadly, neither do the children they've shoved through the meat grinder. It's up to Han and Leia to populate the future of *Star Wars*, or Merry and Pippin to take what they learned during the war and try to apply that logistical know-how and courage/pluck to the practical matters of raising cabbage and mediating with the Tooks and the Proudfeet. The support characters build something. The protagonists smile, wanly, as the adrenaline fades and the scars tighten the skin around their hearts, fading into a world of ghosts.

They have no role to play in peacetime. They were never taught how. There was no time. Destiny demanded it. Destiny called.

---

1. Or don't picture life as a war.

PART FOUR:
Children's Television

Humbled by a Dog

DUNKING ON BAD SHOWS FOR kids is a bit like shooting fish on a plate.[1] Most children's programming is absolute horseshit. Big, fat turds that plop out indiscriminately. It is predatory, leveraging the fact that kids are psychologically attracted to repetition, bright colours, simplistic paradigms, fewer variables, cardboard characters, canned dialogue bordering on catchphrases, and inevitably married to rabid marketing and merchandising campaigns, harnessing little kids' inability to separate fiction from reality and desire from need. I hate it. I hate myself for letting my kid watch television, for owning a television, and not spending every spare moment going for walks in the woods.

At the same time, I recognize that there is a need to inoculate my son against the depravities of our culture. I don't think it's worked, because, well, because I don't have a heart of stone.

Early on, my son fell for the great kid trap of our age: *PAW Patrol*. When we started to give him some agency over the slice of television he gets to watch, he asked for it almost religiously. Now, I totally understand that a singular devotion to

---

1. *Even easier* than shooting fish in a barrel.

a particular franchise is a very common experience that some might even say is formative. I can recall my nephew's fascination with Elmo, alongside a previous subgeneration of tots. But *PAW Patrol* is the worst. No story, just a Pavlovian chain of stimulus rendered through single-variable problem-solving. Need a boulder moved? There's a construction pup for that. Need a ladder? Firefighter pup will hook you up. Ad nauseam.

When I tried to steer him in another direction around age 1.5 or so, I sat my son down and asked him, point-blank, "Why do you like *PAW Patrol*?"

He said, "Makes L— happy."

I ... I had no counter-argument. I'd prefer if he watched something like *Puffin Rock* or *Peppa Pig*, which at least tried to have stories and characters, rather than obtuse problem-solving matrices, but he *liked PAW Patrol*. It made him happy. Who was I to contest that? To deny his emotional reality?

So, sure, I worry about the seeming right-wing propaganda embedded in a show where every social service is overseen by a private enterprise of a boy who has six puppies driving trucks, but I've resigned myself to the fact that *PAW Patrol* will stick around until my son bores of it.

•

The kind of scary meta thing is that the vast bulk of preschooler shows are just the lowest-effort pap competing for attention through overstimulation and taking advantage of the fact that (a) children's brains are underdeveloped and (b) the specific spice of that underdevelopment has never been understood better. What that means is that the structural essence of these shows is predicated on a methodology that makes them abhorrent to adults.

These shows really are built for two audiences, and instead of leveraging that psychological insight, they prey on it. They make shows in such a way that they mesmerize kids, making them want more and more and more, teaching them to binge from the age of two.

It also means that these shows are literal hell for parents to watch, which further inculcates the freakish duality of plopping kids in front of a television while the parent takes care of something else. Look, it happens. We're all ashamed of it, but we've also all been alone and needed to make dinner. I understand the limitations of the individual parent, and wish no shame or ill will upon anyone for taking advantage of half an hour of scripted kiddie junk. I just hate *myself* for it, and hate the programs for being so godawful. I hate seeing my son clearly in that moment, zombie eyes half-lidded, sitting alone on the couch, sucking at the teat of a garbage funnel of Day-Glo nonsense literally screamed at him at the top of the television's lungs.

Thank goodness for shows like *Sesame Street, Daniel Tiger's Neighborhood, StoryBots*, and others built off an educational paradigm. They may be just as addictive as the rest, just as ready a ramp toward a little goober gobbling up the soma of television, but at least there's kindness and numbers, awareness and the alphabet, peppered here and there among the Muppets.

This is also why parents love Pixar so much. The colour palette and narrative clarity[1] appeals to kids, and the story is at least *a story*, so kids *and* adults can all sit together for an hour and a half.

But what do you do when your kid is too young to enjoy those movies? When their brain is still forming the necessary links of causality that allow a clear narrative structure to crank their interest-chain?

Enter *Peppa Pig*. Because I am someone who (a) has been employed in all manner of weird ways that provide some measure of flexibility with my time; (b) has a morbid fascination

---

1. The oft-cited Pixar story structure is as clear as glass: Once upon a time there was [blank]. Every day, [blank]. One day [blank]. Because of that, [blank]. Until finally [blank].

with media while also loathing it (and, let's be honest, loathing myself a bit for being fascinated by it); and (c) totally understands that sometimes a parent needs to cut the vegetables and a television set is a useful attention panacea — the cocktail that arises is one wherein I want to inspect the drug by pushing a bit of it through my own spiritual bloodstream first. So I try to watch as many of L—'s shows as I can. To talk about them with him. To make sure that the abhorrent depictions of socialization are kept to a minimum, or at the very least were things we could counter with example and modelling.

Now that my wife has picked up a good deal of the parenting slack (we recently swapped who was working more and who was parenting more), when she says that a show is "Not terrible. At least decent," that is a gosh darn diamond in the rough. And that's what *Peppa Pig* was, alongside a handful of other shows we discovered on various streaming platforms — like *Puffin' Rock* (worth it for the animation style and rockin' watercolour backgrounds, not to mention Chris O'Dowd's narration. Unfortunately, the show doesn't really offer much for the greater dad bod conversation) — that we wanted our son to watch, rather than the crystal core problem shows (like *PAW Patrol* [1] or this terror junk on YouTube [2]) that he really

---

1. There was a time we were afraid to even say the name out loud in case L— heard us and demanded satisfaction like a musketeer.

2. I am not equipped to deal with this problem. These "animations" are even more distilled brain bleach than crappy television shows, and are starting to show up on streaming services. Low budget CG animation without any textures, the smooth, frictionless bodies of these terrible shorts and songs have an uncanny appeal to the toddler mind, which is still pretty enraptured by high contrast imagery. Stay the heck away if you can. These unshows are the artistic equivalent of feeding your child bits of broken glass in a Ziploc bag full of salt and sugar. If you have a grotesque curiosity to sate, check out "Learn Colors With Cars and Trucks | Street Vehicles In Cargo | Cars Colors Videos For Kids" from the YouTube channel Kids Channel – Cartoon Videos for Kids, all of which was written by an SEO bot. Or any "Hey Bear Sensory" videos. My son was particularly fond of the Funky Veggies Dance.

wanted to watch, because they executed so perfectly on that predatory design platform.

So we watched some *Peppa Pig*, a cute little British show made up entirely of pinks and greys, with 2-D cut-out-looking characters and a veritable host of dad bod problems.

Peppa's dad is fat. Everyone comments on this constantly. He is also bad at everything. People poke fun at this. His children poke fun at this. I'm not sure if an entire episode has gone by where someone doesn't at least (a) make fun of his stomach/weight, or (b) heavily doubt his ability to do totally normal activities, like riding a bicycle or going for a walk in the rain.

Peppa's dad has a '90s developer goatee. All straggles of maggoty hair clinging onto his face with no true beardy conglomeration. It is a very weird design choice, and further leads me to believe that the creators of *Peppa Pig* hate fathers categorically.

Peppa's dad gets no respect. Rodney Dangerfield levels of no respect. Despite the fact that he actually has a position of relative authority, not only in his job but in his field. What's crazy is that the show actually went out of its way to highlight Daddy Pig's renown in an episode where the Pig family takes a train to Continental Europe, and it's revealed that Daddy Pig is a pseudo-celebrity because of his groundbreaking work in cement and infrastructural design. Like the entire train full of people going to this industry conference, and maybe even some regular people who have heard about innovations in concrete, are straight-up asking for his autograph and fawning over him. It's wild. This man is well-respected in the field of concrete. This Pig is the Ivan Locke of concrete in the world of *Peppa Pig*. And yet it amounts to literally nothing the next time some parent or child, or his own children, in-laws, or brother discuss his inability to open a can of soup.

•

The dad bod of *Peppa Pig* is a goddamn travesty. He takes all of the lumps of the bumbling Sitcom Dad, despite having the skills and abilities of the Distant Driven Dad, and he's actually present(!) for the family's outings and needs. If it was only the case that he was respected by *anyone* around him, that would actually play into a kind of old-school, Atticus Finch kind of dad who takes those lumps and shoulders that burden silently, or with good-natured British stiff upper lip.

But *Peppa Pig* utterly undermines this possibility due to the fact that it shows us that everyone's disrespect of Daddy Pig is warranted. He is pretty bad at basic tasks. He messes stuff up constantly. He is pretty unaware, both of himself and others. He is, for lack of a better term, a basic bumbling British dad, with virtually no redeeming qualities except for the fact that he's present.

That's not nothing, but it is a pretty crap representation.

Like my wife said, it's not terrible.

The only reason I'm writing about it — because, let's face it, Daddy Pig is a fairly bog-standard dad bod — is that *Peppa Pig* gave indirect birth to the greatest contemporary dad bod: Bandit from *Bluey*.

.

Joe Brumm, thank you. From the bottom of my soul. Thank you for showing it can be done. Someone can make a piece of successful commercial children's entertainment that connects to true human experience.

Joe Brumm is an animator from Australia who proved his bona fides in the U.K. on award-winning kids' shows like *Charlie and Lola*. When he went back to Brisbane, he started a small animation studio that got gigs and paid the bills but wasn't pushing the needle. In interviews, Brumm notes a basic disgust with children's programming as I outlined above: it's repetitive, it's formulaic, it isn't doing anything fun, and it's almost impossible for parents and children to enjoy the same show. Worst of all — it isn't *real*. And though there are outrageous settings and fantastic seeming set-ups, there isn't the true spice of imagination to a lot of these shows. There's nothing weird, and certainly nothing as weird as the totally bonkers concepts that actual kids come up with on the regular.

So Brumm went around trying to pitch *Bluey*, as both a kind of "Australian *Peppa Pig*" but also, and I'm being dead serious here, an anti–*Peppa Pig* of the highest artistic calibre.

Bluey is, like *Peppa*, a show about anthropomorphic animals living in a simulacrum of our world. That is pretty much where the comparison ends. I can understand how it would've been a useful pitch to get through the first five seconds of a conversation with a television executive, especially considering *Peppa*'s global appeal, but unlike *Peppa*, where every element seems to reinforce boring stereotypes and even more boring situations, *Bluey* is on another level in every single way.

Let's start with the premise: anthropomorphic animals. In *Peppa*, each family is a different animal. There's the Pigs, the Rabbits, and so on, each main character named with alliterative patterns to tickle a toddler's ears. Suzy Sheep, Pedro Pony, Danny Dog, etc. What's peculiar is that, when you look closely at this arrangement, there is no unification among the populace. They are all different animals. How do they breed? Do you have to look for another pig? There are no mixes. It's a stratified society.

Not so in *Bluey*, because they are all dogs. Sure, different families might be different breeds, but there is nothing stopping breeds from mixing it up. That means that there is built-in diversity among the individuals that you see throughout the show, and the dog-people are conscious about those superficial breed differences, while also sharing an overarching commonality: they're all dogs. Just like we're all people.

Bluey follows the Heeler family, all blue heelers, which is a common Australian breed. There's the children, Bluey (six years old) and Bingo (four years old), and the parents — Chilli, the mom, and Bandit, the dad.

Bandit is *the* dad bod. Bandit is a better dad than me. There, I said it. Bandit is probably a better dad than anyone on the planet. Sure, as a kids' show character he inevitably has his most negative burrs sanded off, but *Bluey* does not in any way, shape, or form shy away from how extremely hard and exhausting parenting is. The cartoon is not afraid to show Bandit and Chilli making real mistakes and owning up to them with their kids. Straight-up, the portrayal of Bandit is nothing short of revolutionary in the world of fatherhood. And the crazy thing is, Brumm (who writes every single one of the so-far over a hundred episodes of the show) based Bandit on the real dads he knows.

That's all it took. Opening up your eyes and looking around. Even if our shows haven't, dads have evolved.

That's the secret of *Bluey*. The show tries to depict real kids, real parents, and real parenting situations, and model the real behaviour, insights, and understanding that we have with regards to the development of little people.

It's so simple, and so powerful, because, like all great art, every piece of *Bluey* contributes to a whole greater than the sum of its parts.

The writing is incredible. The stories are efficiently told, hilarious, down to earth, and full of imagination. They show the incredible *Monty Python*–esque fluid reality that children live in, and they're brimming with emotional impact and real parenting lessons.

The art direction is stupendous. *Peppa Pig* looks like a lazy undergrad's weekend project when they ran out of time between benders. In *Bluey*, each scene is crafted with stunning, vivacious intensity — it feels like the way kids see the world, with brighter colours and bolder shapes, with a kind of visual wonder that only exists the first time a child witnesses something. Whether it is the Heelers' house, a backwoods creek, or a downtown Chinese restaurant, the backgrounds are rendered with wonderful little details that anchor the imaginary space in a rock-solid verisimilitude.

The voice acting is off the charts. The kids are voiced by real kids, split between child actors and the kids of the production crew. In fact, the kids are uncredited, to protect their identities. This gives the characters an incredible vocal range and presence completely unlike adults pretending to be kids with high-pitched warbling. The kids' voices break, they have weird rhythms and diction, and if you've been around kids then that fricative aural friction resonates with an authenticity that cuts to the emotional quick. And Bandit is voiced by David McCormack, front man of Australian indie-rock band Custard, who says that he doesn't put on a voice for the role.

With each creative decision, that double adherence to reality *and* imagination blends what ought to be binaries into a single, cohesive whole. And the show *delivers*. It *slaps*.

Take a look at how *Bluey* models parenting: The core conceit of the show is play. The importance of play. The self-guided learning that children undergo in unstructured play. Bandit and Chilli go out of their way to reinforce and go along with the playful realities that their children develop, all of which ring with the clarion of truth because they are based on actual games that Brumm's two daughters drag him into. (We'll get back to this later.)

The whole show is based upon him hanging out with his kids. Of course it is going to tower head and shoulders over some nonsense devised in a writers room by poltroons intent on sucking the eyeball juice out of toddlers.

·

Now that we've got the lay of the land, let's dive into the dad bod of Bandit, the paragon of fatherhood.

By the numbers: he's an active caregiver, working from home in order to spend more time with his kids, to be a part of their lives, to help raise them, to be a part of their emotional world, to help them with conflict, and, more than anything else, to play with them.

He's also a modern partner: he doesn't just do the dishes and the laundry, make food, change diapers, clean the house, and do the shopping — he does them *happily*, understanding that they aren't chores, they aren't infringements upon his free time, or upon his agency, or upon his status as a man — no, these are the things that help make life worth living. Not the reward, per se, not the quick of life, but rather the deeds you do to have a nice life. Bandit shows, in pretty much every episode, that there is no domestic task so onerous that you can't have a little fun while doing it. This is so subtly rendered and so gigantically huge I want to take a big red marker and circle this paragraph over and over again in every copy of this book.[1] As soon as men dispense with the idea that household chores are somehow thrust upon them, as soon as they stop treating their wives like their bosses when it comes to the tasks that we (we!) need to do around the house, as soon as that ressentiment is dropped like the idiotic hot potato that it is, we will be so, so much closer to doing away with a massive chunk of sexist hangover that continues to afflict so much of North American discourse on masculinity.

Like, men seem to believe they are somehow above domestic work. Still. I know that sounds zany as heck, but I also know that while I was growing up my mother made 90 percent or more of our family meals and that it was just sort of assumed

---

1. If you bought a version like that, I'm super sorry. Sometimes I can't help myself.

that would continue to be the case forever. It wasn't questioned, it wasn't even voiced, and even though my dad explicitly cares a great deal about equality, it wasn't until recently[1] that he started picking up the slack. By the same token, my sister was taught how to cook, around the age of ten. I wasn't. I lived, until pretty recently, with an extremely basic set of culinary skills and recipes that I clung to with the fervour of a zealot. I could not improvise, I could not think for myself when it came to stoves, and I was so scared of wasting food that the idea of deviating gave me palpitations and conniptions.

I wanted to cook my half of family meals, as I want to do my obvious share with everything, but eating the same five meals over and over again was a straight-up nightmare for my wife. I was fulfilling the letter of the law but not the spirit of it, like some kind of petulant teenager, and it was fear that held me back from trying new recipes and stretching beyond the capacities that I already possessed.

That doesn't jive with parenthood.

Bandit dives headfirst into that spirit — of blasting into the unknown, trying new ideas out, iterating, learning from mistakes — all of those good practices that coincide with not only modern parenting, but also modern business practice and learning theories.

The core of which is play. Again and again we see the wonderful capacity for play to teach, to engage, to grant agency and spur autonomous thought, to connect us, to provide a safe narrative space for emotional expression and working through our fears — play is a superpowerful tool.

And it is Bandit and Chilli's parenting superpower.

When my wife first sat down to watch *Bluey*, it seemed to her like the show might be about Australian dog kids with

---

1. When he retired before she did, I think, was the impetus.

magic powers. (It isn't.) That's how hard Bandit plays into the children's imagination games. The first episode, "Magic Xylophone," is about Bluey and her sister, Bingo, rediscovering a "magic xylophone" at the bottom of their toy chest. Every time Bluey hits one of the xylophone's clarion metal tones, Bandit pretends to freeze in space and time.

"Sure," you say. "Freeze tag or whatever, I've played that game before."

No. You haven't. Not like this.

When Bandit pretends to wake up from that first freeze, he acts all groggy and confused, slowly catching on to what's going down in the same way you would if you intermittently blacked out while your children were playing hilarious pranks on you.[1] No matter what else is going on, when his kids hit the xylophone, Bandit *freezes*. Doesn't matter if Bluey and Bingo are sticking his finger up his nose, drawing wackadoo spectacles and mustachios on his face, or forcing him to hold a gushing garden hose up to his own head — Bandit leans into the rules of the game and holds fast. The commitment that he has to his kids' play is incomprehensible — and yet that is exactly what real parents do, albeit on a different scale.

Think about playing hide-and-seek with any kid who is a little bit too young to totally understand the game. My toddler is pretty good at hiding, but, still, you ham it up. You make sure to look in at least a few places where you know they aren't hiding, narrating what you're doing, not only to help establish the rules of the game, but also to help build the suspense of being found out, which is the true fun of the game. *Bluey* takes this core concept and applies it to a myriad of inventive situations cut from the cloth of real life.

---

1. Which, honestly, is not that different from parenting in the fugue state of hyper sleep deprivation.

The incredible side effect of Bandit's play-conviction is that it solidifies the reality of the rules for the kids, too. Back in "Magic Xylophone," Bandit pulls the ole switcharoo on Bluey and swipes the xylophone while Bluey and Bingo are arguing over whose turn it is. Bandit hits the xylophone and Bluey freezes, playing with just as much conviction as her father. In mock retribution he sets her up as a gnome in the garden and threatens to spray her with a hose to clean her off. Throughout this exchange, Bluey isn't quite as convincing about being frozen (she is mumbling through a rictus frown) *but she doesn't blow the game* and instead stands there awaiting her goofy punishment. Even more, after Bingo gets the magic xylophone and "unfreezes" Bluey for the core moral moment of the episode,[1] and even though Bluey doesn't have to, *she freezes again perfectly* when Bingo turns the tides on her sister in order to explain that it hurts Bingo's feelings when Bluey doesn't give her an opportunity to play in the make-believe.

They reconcile and agree to take turns. When Bandit comes back with the garden hose in tow, Bluey pretends to still be frozen so Bingo can have an opportunity to ambush Bandit with one final freeze. Bluey delivers my favourite line of the episode to a frozen Bandit holding the hose up to his own face: "We tricked you! Bingo unfroze me, I was just pretending."

The rules are sacrosanct. They make the make-believe.

Contained within this bonkers fun time is a smorgasbord of incredible parenting and child-sized life lessons. Taking turns is important. Supporting your children's play reaps surprising rewards. Leaning into the game is a more fun way of living. Clear emotional communication works. Give kids the tools they need and they'll figure things out on their own.

---

1. Bluey took all the turns freezing their father, despite Bingo's frequent protests that she wanted a turn, too.

And that's all just from the first episode.

They crammed all of that into *seven freaking minutes*.

With fifty-two episodes a season, two seasons in, and with such a stunningly straightforward premise ripe with pleasing variation, the show can afford to be luxuriously generous in the kinds of content that it plays with, and the kinds of situations that the Heeler family encounters.

Like "Keepy Uppy," the third episode and as perfect a pitch as you can imagine for a show like this as it is pure, unmitigated fun. The premise is so simple and straightforward: they're playing with a balloon. They're playing the game we've all played with a balloon at some point in time, a game so primally attached to the concept of balloons that I honestly wonder whether it was the reason that balloons were invented. That's right, whatever you called it, the game where you do everything in your human powers to make sure that the balloon does not touch the floor.

Each time they hit the balloon, Bandit makes it a little bit harder for the girls to get under it, eventually using a leaf blower to send the balloon on a madcap tour of the entire house *and* providing a clean visual metaphor for the way that play pushes children's boundaries and helps them learn how to work harder. What's more, the ramping up of balloon-hitting-stakes also mirrors the tempo of madness that comes with child-play: if left to their own devices, that crescendo will continue to build and build until something breaks or someone gets hurt. All of these lessons bundled up in life's most basic balloon game.

Episode after episode, *Bluey*'s core commitment to play and a kind of emergent parenting coupled with the equitable co-parenting and creative mediation of conflict somehow provide hit after hit like the early Beatles. Or Radiohead. How do they keep doing it over and over again? Each and every time you are blown away by the risks they are willing to take and the virtuosity that the animation studio employs in going straight for the jugular.

Take "Fruitbat," one of my favourite early episodes. In it, Bluey doesn't want to go to sleep. Instead she wants to be a fruit bat. After a few swift scenes where Bandit uses games to help convince the girls to go to bed, and the depiction of a healthy bedtime ritual, there is a quick scene when Bluey can't fall asleep and her dad, exhausted from a day of parenting, is passed out on the floor, clutching a rugby ball, doing that thing dogs do when they run and kick with their legs as they sleep, play-growling and the like. Bluey asks her mom what's up with dad. Chilli says that Bandit's dreaming about playing touch football with his mates, which is something that he both loves to do and doesn't get to do much anymore, so instead he dreams about it. When Bluey asks why he doesn't get to play it for real life, Chilli says that it's because he's too busy, "working and looking after you two." This information is met with a quiet "oh," as Bluey tries to process, briefly, what that must be like for her dad. Then she gets the idea of dreaming being a fruit bat, gets excited about going to sleep (which is great kid logic), and has a trippy dream about being a bat. In the dream she continues to process that drop of empathetic information about her father, and sees him with his mates — an individual rather than an extension of her care. The next morning, she goes out of her way to thank her father for taking care of her. Just this tiny little moment, on the outside, that acts as an indicator for all of the incredible growth of a little person brewing just under the surface.

Even more pleasing is the fact that the show has managed to stay fresh despite the sheer volume of content because, unlike almost every other children's show I've been forced to sit through, *Bluey* does not stick to any conventional pattern, layout, or narrative arc. Some episodes are downright experimental in their pacing and structure.

"Takeaway" is a perfect example, an ever-escalating crescendo of madness that highlights all of the hijinks that little kids can get up to in five minutes when you really, really need them to *just sit still*. Or "Bike," which breaks down different kids trying and failing at different exercises around the playground, in an Eisensteinian montage of iterative play and the power of perseverance with the rhythmic intercutting of an old Daft Punk music video. However, if I was going to have to choose my favourite for this structural point, it would have to be "Chickenrat," which is completely unfair because it juggles three narrative layers simultaneously.

The frame narrative for "Chickenrat" is retracing Bingo's and Bluey's steps in order to help teach the kids how to jog their memory, since Bingo misplaced her bedtime stuffy. So the episode is told in hilarious backward leaps through their evening adventures, which include magic wands, ninja costumes, a restaurant game, and an elaborate scheme to get the egg of the titular chimera.[1] This pseudo-reverse chronological ordering to the episode highlights the internal logic of the kids' play, while simultaneously building up the mystery that propels the episode's plot and allows it to unfold in a way that brings us even closer to the child's perspective. A lost toy might seem trivial to us, but it is both mystifying and properly distressing to a child — especially with the looming deadline of bedtime. Throughout, the shift in coloration of the evening provides an immediate visual cue for what time of day it is in this nonlinear story, a technique that would make it so that, conceivably, even a preschooler would be able to follow along.

---

1. Which their dad invented when they asked him to play the restaurant game, in order to give him a few more minutes reading the newspaper.

Back to Bandit. Yes, there's more. This cartoon dog has more depth than any dad bod we've looked at so far. There's so, so much more.

One thing that Bandit and Chilli try to do, and succeed at admirably the majority of the time, is be fully present with their children. I don't mean that they are never distracted, or never have some overarching concern on their mind — in fact, the tension that emerges when you need to get out the door in five minutes and your child is demanding that they are, in fact, a frog, so they cannot walk right now, that's some of the main meat in the conflict between parent and child in the show. How a child's frame of priorities is just so fundamentally disconnected from the logistical necessities that drive most adult decision-making and, you know, making it through a real day.

Again, "Takeaway" is a great example of this disconnected framing. When picking up their takeout Chinese food, Bandit is obviously beat after a long day with these two rapscallion daughters. He just wants to get through this moment of waiting for the restaurant to finish making the family's dinner. He wants the kids to "be good," which translates to, in essence, "not take up any of Daddy's bandwidth." They can't. They're kids. They can't turn off the wonder that they experience from the world. They can't turn off the questions they have about everything they see.[1] And, central to this whole zany episode, they can't stop being kids. They can't stop wanting to play, wanting to explore, wanting to get inside the marrow of life. They aren't being bad when they goof around, even if they aren't being obedient, either. Reconciling the distance between obedience and goodness is central to raising toddlers

---

1. So well-captured in this episode is Bingo's relentless four-year-old curiosity. "Why do we eat some plants and not others?" "If grown-ups grow from babies, and only grown-ups have babies, who had the first baby?"

and preschoolers, and central to understanding the magic of *Bluey*'s play-based philosophy.

So no, it's not that those global concerns don't exist — *Bluey* isn't a fantasy in the sense that Bandit isn't concerned with totally normal for-real priorities like dinners and bath time, just the opposite! So many episodes burrow down deep into the absolute bog-standard details of life: going to a big box store, grocery shopping, figuring out how to deal with a parent working from home, coming to terms with missing a parent who isn't there, going camping, playing at the playground — it's all drawn from the time parents spend with their children. Even though it isn't fantastic (in the sense of most boring kid shows that take place in totally unreal situations without any psychological or environmental weight) it is *magical*, because these parents try to find the magic of each moment with their kids, whenever they can. They find that magic by being present, by paying as much attention as they can, by letting their children lead, and by believing in the realities that their children present. First and foremost the central emotional reality each child inhabits, followed by the playful realities that expand and collapse with Bluey's and Bingo's creative rhythms.

It's not that Bandit and Chilli don't talk to other adults, or even talk to other adults about adult subjects, or, to really draw the point home, talk about things outside the scope of their children's understanding — but they don't do so when the kids are talking to them. They don't ever act as though their kids don't exist. And you know what? That's *hard*.

I'm still working through a bunch of my own shit, as a person halfway through this saunter from the maternity ward to the crematorium. I have all kinds of issues and problems that crop up during the day that I want to talk to my wife about. Dinnertime used to be when we would have at least half an hour to cut through some of that noise and connect to one another, get a bit of a barometer reading on how we were doing, and figure out what we could do that evening to help, to plan, to talk, to work, to play — in order to recreate ourselves and make it through to the next day. It wasn't perfect, but it was a process.

Now, with my son there, it feels wrong for us to do that deep dive. When we do, because sometimes the internal feedback loop is shooting off too many sparks, I always feel rotten afterward because it's like I completely ignored his existence for the ten minutes that I'm yammering on about whatever topical nonsense is scudding through my cortex. When I'm lucky, I realize halfway through and curtail the discussion for another time. When I'm not, I realize afterward, and find myself doing double duty trying to kickstart a conversation about what he learned at preschool or the games he played today with Mommy.

I don't see that with Bandit, and I can only imagine that the choice to not include this kind of quotidian griping is yet another conscious artistic decision in this oh-so-intentional show. The thing is, Bandit's an archaeologist. That's right, this dog's a professional with a graduate degree. From the archaeologists I know, archaeology is less of a career and more of a calling. It is the kind of work that you don't do for the glory, or the money, or the adventure — you do it because it is a passion, or because a part of your soul lives in the gap stretched between eras and epochs, a kind of extended historical awareness that spans hundreds, if not thousands, of years.

So you might think that archaeology would be pouring out of Bandit all the time, and yet he never brings his work into the children's lives. He's never going on and on about a dig or a conference or a recent paper that's blown up in the field. He does work from home, we do get to see inside his office, and there are other, subtle hints that he is well-versed in history and myth,[1] but Bandit doesn't take his work home with him. That is a *feat*.

Instead, and this sounds a bit understated so I'm going to have to juice it up as we go, Bandit's primary role is Daddy. What I mean is, the archaeologist part of his persona is irrelevant to his children. It doesn't even enter into the picture. This can be pretty hard to fathom sometimes, given how much bandwidth our careers and ambitions take up inside our heads — but that's the important barrier: it's all inside our heads. Sure, it's also what we spend the vast majority of our waking hours doing, and those modalities and methodologies undoubtedly contribute to a subtle (or not) reshaping of our bodies and minds in order to become more effective and efficient at our role and industry of choice, but I cannot emphasize enough how that has absolutely no bearing on the qualities and characteristics that go into being a solid parent.

This is extremely hard for me to parse. I am the kind of person who is obsessively consumed by the work I do. When I realized that I wanted to become a writer about ten years ago, I stopped doing everything else. Much to the detriment of my life, personal growth, and writing! I have inappropriately grafted my identity and self-picture onto pretty much every job that I have ever entertained, which is a big part of the reason why I have such a mixed professional background — I kept trying to brute-force each occupation into a calling or a full bastion of self, when, at most, it should have only participated in a fraction of my selfhood. All of my self-worth was confined to the quality and quantity of words published per month. It was a great tool

---

1. In the second episode, "Hospital," where Bluey and Bingo pretend to extract a cat from Bandit's stomach, when they ask for the patient's name he says, without waiting a beat, "Telemachus." And in the lovely episode about playing in nature, "The Creek," the children make-believe that the pool of water is a day spa, and he calls Bingo "Cassiopeia."

for forcing me to think and act strategically and professionally, but it was also a surefire track to burnout and alienation.

When my wife and I had our son, the last vestiges of that illusion went out the window. Here was a little person whose sole understanding of me was as an extension of their family. I am L—'s daddy. That is who I am to him. That's all I am to him. My work, my life, that entire leviathan of struggle and confusion, does not and should not exist for him. Instead, I am the guy who makes him breakfasts. I am the warm body to snuggle with in the night when he is beset with "scary black balls" that rise up out of the carpet in his room at one in the morning. I am someone he can hide from his mother with, giggling under the covers. I am a partner for walks in the woods. I am someone who holds and kisses his mother. I am someone who picks him up from preschool. I am a companion on adventures to the playground. I am someone who can kiss his wounds and hold him through tears, and who listens to everything he says. I am a source of information, security, play, and love.

I am his daddy.

That's what matters. The rest is moot. For him. For my relationship with him. What matters is what we do when we're together. What matters is that we make the time to do it.

Bluey gets that, hard. Within the context of interactions with his children, Bandit is first and foremost a father — no, he is first and foremost *their* father. And even though he has a life outside of that, or he used to, that isn't what's important anymore. They are.

That's what being a parent is. Being present. Being aware. Being there. However, whenever, to whatever extent you can.

·

Returning to "Fruitbat" briefly, when Chilli tells Bluey that her dad doesn't have time to play touch football with his mates anymore because he's too busy with work and "taking care of you two" — that tiny line carries so much weight. It is delivered without judgment or resentment, but instead a kind of pragmatic straight-shooting that is remarkable. Telling a six-year-old that raising kids is hard work, that it demands a re-prioritization of your life, that things change irrevocably *and that's okay*, better than okay, that parenting is an invaluable trade that broadens the scope of your existence,[1] that is a remarkably courageous and trusting act. Telling a kid that, so directly, is empowering them, and it is one of the many life-sized bits of wisdom that I hope to take away from thinking and writing about this show, and this arc of dad bod analysis.

Way back at the beginning of this book I mentioned that I was expecting to get struck by some kind of internal lightning when I had a kid. That I had assumed it would change me all of a sudden, but instead I felt like I was the same fool with the same idiotic desires and limitations. That's all true. Having a kid doesn't suddenly turn you into a better, or even different, person.

But it does give you an opportunity to do so. A chance to step up and start to own every aspect of your life, to live as much of it as you can with intention, because now you are modelling the value and meaning of life to a little person who has a sponge of a brain and is lapping up *everything*. Sure, you've got a bit of a ramp to get up to speed, as different segments of your child's brain kick on every few months after birth, but that is also the time when you will really get to know yourself and (if you're lucky enough to have one during this experience) your partner. No sleep. No time. Improvising every day for the next twenty years. It is a challenge, and it's up to you whether you want to make it a grind, or a dance. A job, or a game.

---

1. If you'll forgive me waxing a bit about parenthood.

What do you do when you are beat, out of resources, and the demand for real connection is right there, staring at you?

Bluey rests squarely on one side of that debate, and I can't help but agree.

.

Even with this incredible pedigree, of the show and of Bandit as a father, it's absolutely essential to note that *Bluey* does not portray him as perfect. Bandit may be dad bod of the year, and an incredible step forward for a contemporary representation of fatherhood and masculinity,[1] but he also makes mistakes. Both Bandit and Chilli are shown in a number of episodes as making real blunders with respect to their children. They hurt their kids' feelings. They allow externalities and status quo to get in the way of the present moment. They don't always respect their kids' boundaries. They squabble with the kids. They get upset themselves. And, sometimes, no matter how hard they try, sometimes they don't listen to Bluey and Bingo.

But they never lose their temper. And as soon as they realize what they've done, they apologize. They own up to it. They explain where they're coming from and why it happened. They treat their little kids like little people, rather than like dogs. Understanding trumps obedience. And in respect of their children's emotional realities, they treat their kids' emotional injuries as real as they are — rather than brushing them aside for expediency.

_____

1. I forgot to mention, despite being emotionally aware and capable at domestic chores and sharing emotional labour and co-parenting, Bandit is a straight-up "mate." He likes rugby and touch football. The most fun he has that isn't playing with his kids is barbecuing and ripping some stumps out of the ground. He is not really a political portrayal, but is, in fact, rather normal. He's a revolution of a figure, of a dad bod, but a totally normal guy in terms of almost all bog-standard scans of traditional masculinity. He just isn't riddled with insecurity and sexism.

Straight-up, Bandit messes up hard a few times, and *Bluey* is stronger for showing it. In "The Dump" Bluey finds out that her father's been recycling her crayon drawings. She cries, because of course it'd feel terrible if your dad treated something you worked really hard on as literal garbage. What's worse, he has obviously been hiding it from her. Bluey and Bingo call their father a baddie,[1] and rescind their previous award of "Best Dad Ever." Bandit apologizes. He explains that Bluey makes so much art, they can't keep it all. He offers to not throw it out. And, when Bluey says that it hurts that he was going to toss it in with all the yucky garbage, it offers Bandit an opportunity to explain how recycling works. Surprisingly, Bluey likes the idea of new paper coming from old paper. She likes the idea of another kid getting to draw on it. Of being part of a larger ecosystem. And she forgives her father.

Sure, it's a bit of a conceit, but the underlying methodology is sound: own up to your mistakes, listen to what bothers other people, talk about it frankly. That is such a sound style of conflict resolution, and unlike the vast majority of the show, it doesn't hinge on the power of imagination or play — but is informed by the same back and forth, give and take, working through issues together that rests at the core of all those games and make-believe stories.

•

Even though *Bluey* makes a very strong argument for play — as a creative tool, as a problem-solving tool, as a conflict-resolution model, as a model for parenting, as a philosophy for life — the show does not shy away from the fact that parenting is raw and exhausting. In the same way that it doesn't pull any punches when it comes to the powerful emotional reality of children

---

1. Prompted by an ad for a superhero movie.

by crawling inside their perspective on life, so too does it not pull any punches when it says that *being a parent is hard work.* This is a remarkable line to balance. Play is fun, right? Play is that space where time disappears and we enter the zone and we float a foot off the ground. Sure, but not for you. Not always. Oh no, that's for the kids. For you, it comes when you want nothing more than to lie down, after a day of juggling spreadsheets and assholes in the passing lane, spilling coffee on your shirt before a big presentation, finding out the sandwiches you want are sold out at the café, being chewed out by your boss or getting a passive-aggressive email from the marketing department, sprinting through the grocery store, chopping vegetables and tossing them in oil, being splash-zoned at bath time while desperate for bedtime — never at the ready, never well-rested, never on point.

Parenting finds you with your figurative pants down, over and over again, and rising to the occasion means being able to *be there anyway,* to try, to find a spark within the cold winter's field of your soul and dig down deeper than you've ever had to before, every single day, because this little person, their view of the world, their day-to-day existence, their philosophy, their sense of self, their emotional well-being, all of it, all of it depends on you nurturing that foundation.

The scope of parenting is unfathomable. Were we to take a four-dimensional view of it, and see the impact and potency of every decision that we made, it would be hard enough to do so with regard to the impact that it has on our own lives. It would be crippling to do so with regard to your kid. We certainly can't retreat from that fact, so we simply have to move on in uncertainty, doing the best we can with the resources that we have available, cobbling together a life that seems worth living.

Again, play makes its affective argument. "Daddy Dropoff" is a painfully real episode. Its narrative structure is seemingly straightforward: get the kids to school on time, with the added twist of an extremely brief framing introduction from a shy puppy we've never seen before. Her name's Lila, and she has a hard time making friends. It's her first day of kindergarten, and instead of talking to the other kids, she builds a Lego wall and hides behind it.

Back in the Heeler house, it's Bandit's turn to take the kids to school, and we know he's doomed from the opening line of "We're not going to be late this time!" as he stomps out of the room with a pair of leashes strapped to each ankle.[1] Commitment to play makes them late: the kids pretend they can't hear Bandit during breakfast, they discover a "slow motion" wand in the yard, and during a prolonged segment in the car Bingo pretends that she is in a house a hundred miles away and Bandit has to call her on the phone to see if she's left her jumper at home (and, therefore, do they have to turn the car around to go and get it) but his imaginary phone keeps calling Bluey instead. Yes, it turns out, the jumper is back home. Tired, frustrated, and anxious about the time, Bandit tries to swiftly drop Bingo off at kindergarten only to hurt her feelings because they didn't play "Wind-up Bingo," a simple game where they pretend Bingo's a little clockwork machine that her Daddy winds up to get her through the front door to school.

You can tell, reading between the lines, that this was one of those games that parents co-create to help their child get through a particular situation. Bandit probably assumed that, like many of the games they play, it would help in that context and then disappear in the wind. Instead, as kids often do, Bingo fixated on it and now it's something she wants whenever she goes through those daunting gates of a place away from her family unit.

---

1. The kids were pretending his feet were pets while he snoozed in bed.

Bandit argues about the time. About how they're late. How he needs to get Bluey to school. Bingo is crestfallen. And it almost seems, for a second, like he might not do it. But then he wouldn't be Bandit. With a sigh, he leans down and puts every ounce of energy and fun and care into his voice as he winds Bingo up and she robot-parades into the kindergarten play space.

When Bluey and Bandit are alone, Bluey asks if winding up Bingo was the difference between them being late or not. No, Bandit admits, they were going to be late either way. It just made them a little bit more late. Then Bluey asks, what would have happened if Bandit didn't wind Bingo up? Well, he muses, she probably would've walked through the doors like normal. "Then why did you do it?" Bandit thinks about it. "I don't know, I just did." Then, when he drops Bluey off at school, he says, "It was more fun, though." Bluey says she's glad he played the game with Bingo. Bandit agrees.

So too does Lila, our shy puppy from the framing at the beginning of the episode, because that's the day she meets Bingo. Chirping like a robot, Bingo mechanically stutters into the classroom in front of the Lego wall Lila is hiding behind. Running out of steam, Bingo slows down, then asks Lila to wind her back up again. Uncertain, the shy pup comes out and mimes winding a big ole key in Bingo's back. When Bingo is unleashed and starts robot-penguin-walking around the room, Lila giggles and joins in, both girls happily trotting around the kindergarten like little maniacs.

"That's how Bingo and I became friends," Lila says overtop of a rapid, and I mean *rapid*, montage of class photos from kindergarten, grade school, high school, and graduation. "I hope we're best friends forever."

The lisping speech patterns of the untrained child actor who plays Lila cuts through me like a knife. I cannot see that montage[1] without misting up. The local and the global unite: without that little bit of play, Bingo would never have met her best friend. Bandit's choice to play "Wind-up Bingo" that one time had untold reverberations in his daughter's life. And it was more fun. It was the right choice to make. It always is.

·

Life is a grind if you make it. Or it can be a wonder-ridden panoply of imagination and joy. The extent to which a parent can pass on that gift of perspective to their children, and all the little things that add up to make life what it is, *Bluey* is all over that.

The show really seems like it has it all. The multi-faceted tool of play, the importance of affirming children's reality and emotions, the potential for a creative solution to life's everyday problems, the opportunity for children and parents to learn from each other at every juncture, the raw representation of the incredibly hard and rewarding work that parenting and partnership is, the portrayal of a competent and emotionally aware father joyfully taking on the emotional and domestic labour that is traditionally modelled in either a hard sexist (doesn't do it) or soft sexist (does it but treats it like a favour) kind of way in the vast majority of mass media, the joy and focus brought into the children's lives through a new approach to the quotidian, the foibles and big emotions that come from looking at life from a child's point of view (taking that on, owning it, not shying away from it, makes *Bluey* a very emotional television-watching experience for a parent of a little one who will soon be embarking on these journeys of self-discovery) ... the fact that it is very good storytelling, that it has a point and an underpinning philosophy that is intentionally woven throughout not only the

---

1. Or the one at the end of "Camping," holy shit. Or "Sleepytime."

narrative details but also the incredible attention to the physical
details of the world it's depicting,[1] that it isn't saccharine, that it
is creative and artistic and structurally experimental in weaving
together content and form, that it is efficient and effective as
all get-out, that it can really be watched and enjoyed by parents
and children simultaneously, that it is drawn awesomely with
charm and character, and that we are getting real people in
every character despite only seeing a tiny vertical slice of them
in any particular moment (but that's actually what it's like to be
human and stumbling around this world where we don't have
interiority with anyone except ourselves) —

It's just so good and so human that it puts almost every
other piece of kid fiction to shame. If I was working on a children's show and I saw *Bluey* I'd either force myself to up my
game or else quit overnight.

.

Remember when I said that my wife thought the show might
be about a magical family of dogs? She was right. Only it wasn't
the crude kind of wizard-magic we tend to think of, but rather
the magic of childhood mixed up with the magic of parenting,
distilled in seven-minute chunks of pure joy, exhaustion, and
heartache.

That sense of everyday magic saturates *Bluey* to such a degree that, upon watching the first few episodes, I had to wonder
"When is all this happening?" Like, is the show only based on
weekends? Or after the kids come home from school? Are they
home-schooled by their father?

Then I pieced it together.

---

1. Just take a look at any toy-strewn playroom shot in the show, or the back seat of
   their car: stickers, crayons, tablets, more stickers, almonds, and pumpkin seeds
   strewn about. Or, in "Fruitbat," the shot of Bingo asleep in full bizarre-kid-yoga-
   pose — these people know kids. They are showing us real life.

The show feels magical, almost magical social realist, be-cause it has captured alive the *feeling* of playing with your kids, which is, truth be told, one of the most magical experiences alive. Especially at this young age when children are still form-ing their metaphysics and the rules of reality are so topsy-turvy, if you can get inside that headspace with them you are opening up a can of pure, uncut wonder, straight from the source.

That magic can happen any time of day, anywhere, when you unleash the shackles of mental bondage and wade into a child's mind-space. The implicit argument of *Bluey* is: any time when you have seven minutes, you can share this magic with your kid.

The idea that this could be any time of day, that any time can be magical, is an incredibly resonant thematic point. As a sleep-deprived parent, it is oh-so-easy to disconnect from the moment and go through the motions. Blandly. Hollowly. As a working parent, it is super easy to get caught up in the guilt that accompanies the awareness that you aren't there at the right times with your child for quality time to happen. Even though there is some truth to that fear, you can still be there for the magic time if you uncork the secret that you can make any time magical as long as you cultivate a sense of wonder and keep your eyes open with every interaction that you have with your kids. They are hungry for it, they are ready for it, just give them a nudge.

This doesn't mean that you need to have the creativity of Joe Brumm, who is, let's be frank, polishing the diamonds of his own real-life experiences with his daughters until they spar-kle with an otherworldly lustre, but you can try to find the play that is within your own capacity and weave the magic that your kids are looking for, even if you only have seven minutes a day with them. Push the exhaustion aside and try to make them laugh the way Bingo and Bluey do almost every single episode.

Uproarious, untethered, overwhelming child-mirth. Be there. It doesn't even have to be some wild play. What matters is showing up. Opening yourself up to your kid's world. That tends to be a world at play because they see the world as play, and they don't have the terrible, torrid associations we do with toil and work. Don't rob them of that perspective prematurely by teaching them that interacting with kids is real work, even though it is. Make it play. Make it a dance. Make it real.

Excuse me while I go cry.

·

The only fictional dad I can really compare Bandit to is Calvin's Dad from *Calvin and Hobbes*.

Calvin's Dad exemplifies so many of the qualities that make Bandit feel more real and three-dimensional than the many dad bods we've encountered, noted, and left behind on this survey of popular culture.

As I said, when I was growing up, Calvin's Dad was a tower of a referent. Here was a fictional dad who I could really, honest-to-goodness see being a real person. He wasn't a straight man for gags, or a bumbling buffoon, or a creation of male power fantasy. He was a regular enough guy, trying to spell out some wisdom for his weirdo son, loving his son despite his eccentricities, holding down a job, having real talk with his partner, holding global — one might even say philosophical — concerns for himself and his family, and generally doing the right thing, despite being a bit of an authoritarian.

Given that it's a comic strip, allow me to provide a few brief, additional flashes of insight into my picture of Calvin's Dad.

A core feature of Calvin's Dad is this idealization he has for the act of camping. Each year he takes his family on a camping trip, and they all hate it. They don't know why he wants to go sleep on a mosquito-infested rock of an island, rather than cozy up in a nice hotel. There's even one strip where Calvin proposes that they do just that: take in some nice spa-type hotel R & R, right, and then *take pictures* to forge evidence that they went camping, like buy a big ole fish at the market and hold it up to look like they had gone camping.

Calvin's Dad is having none of it. The simulacrum isn't the real thing.

In another camping trip, it rains literally the entire time, from the moment they step foot on the island to the second they pack everything back up into the canoe. Everyone tries their best to still have a vacation: they try to go fishing, they try to swim, and each panel is rendered with these really intense vertical slashes of ink to differentiate between the dreadful, constant downpour and the relative safety inside the tent. It is so evocative that I still think about that differentiation every time I crawl into a tent, regardless of the weather.

Let's be real: Nobody enjoys themselves on these trips that the dad forces them to go on. Not even when it's sunny out. When finally confronted, point-blank, why he does this, Calvin's Dad's answer is as revealing as it is a punchline: they go on these trips that are a huge trial and tribulation once a year, roughing it in tents on a rock that they have to paddle out to, scorching in the sun, eating cold beans from a can, fending off mosquitoes the size of hummingbirds — so that the rest of their regular life at home feels like a vacation in comparison.

This comical masochism felt very real to me as a kid, and resonated with the kind of incomprehensible valuation that my parents utilized in their own decision-making. What mattered to them didn't matter to me, and vice versa.

That seemed normal.

Another series of vignettes, *Calvin and Hobbes* places equal pri-
macy on imagination as *Bluey*, albeit with very different constraints. Calvin's Dad is cut from a different cloth than Bandit,
and he does not — I would wager *cannot* — participate in the
robust make-believe games that populate Calvin's days. Nor
does Calvin's Dad, or anyone else in Calvin's life, value them.
As a dad bod, Bandit goes further. He is integrated into his
child's life in a way that Calvin's Dad can't be, because the
focus of each text is so different.

At its core, *Calvin and Hobbes* is about the relationship between a boy and his imaginary tiger — the only true friend
Calvin has because nobody else gets him. Calvin's parents are
side characters whose roles expand along with the thematic ex-
pansion that Watterson explored throughout the comic's ten-
year life cycle. He breathed more life into Calvin's Dad (for
which I'm very thankful) and even placed their relationship at
the centre of a handful of comics, but it was never the soul of
the matter. Its soul was ostracization.

Not so *Bluey*, which is, in its heart, about the integrated
family unit, and Bandit's holistic relationship with the two
children.

Before I saw *Bluey*, I was going to end the book on Calvin's
Dad. He seemed like the only father figure from my past media
experiences who had any solidity or verisimilitude. The rest
were carbon copies of abstract tropes, piecemeal assemblages
of the association between stereotypical masculine identity
and its cumbersome relationship to these little people we have
running all around us. Traditional men have a problem when
it comes to children, exemplified by characters like Captain
Picard[1] who, even though he is expressly a father figure for all
of the thousand or so people aboard the USS *Enterprise*

---

1. Do I even need to say, from *Star Trek: The Next Generation*?

(NCC-1701-D), has some serious discomfort around kids. Each time teen wunderkind Wesley Crusher comes aboard in those first few seasons, Sir Patrick looks like he's simultaneously eating a cockroach and has a bursting need to pee.

Calvin's Dad is a huge step beyond traditional men of that ilk. He is attentive and conversational, interested in his son's well-being, and brimming with a kind of pragmatic stoicism that is well worth unpacking.

The key to Calvin's Dad is his twisted take on authority that we touched on previously. Despite wanting Calvin to listen to him, Calvin's Dad will not reciprocate. Calvin's Dad is more than willing to dispense totally nonsensical lies to play with his son's gullibility, but not to participate in Calvin's imaginary play one jot.

Frustratingly, Calvin's Dad is also pretty unengaged at times. He yells and screams. He shoos Calvin away so he can read the paper or a book. He tries to share experiences or ideas with Calvin, but almost always on the dad's terms: telling Calvin some words of wisdom, showing Calvin how to do something (like play baseball) that Calvin doesn't even want to do, and generally responding to Calvin's instinct to play and imagine with ... maybe not disdain, so much as a rigid adherence to pragmatic reality. Calvin's Dad doesn't do this to be cruel, I don't think, but because he believes (as I think a lot of dads did in the '80s) that it was his primary job to prepare Calvin for "the world," rather than participate in the world alongside his son.

So Calvin's Dad sets himself up as an arbiter and judge on the veracity and value of activities. Certainly, that is a parent's role, especially given how much television kids want to watch, but when it becomes the sum total of your stance as a parent, you create an impoverished relationship that is predicated on a foundation of contrariness and opposition.

Calvin's Dad is Calvin's foil. Since the comic is primarily about the value and beauty of imagination and the imaginative games that Calvin plays with Hobbes, Calvin's Dad is shut out from that ineffable wonder that makes life vital for Calvin. It's a little tragedy bundled up inside an otherwise whimsical romp. We're alongside Calvin. We're there for the ride. His dad isn't. His dad is focused, to a fault, on the fact that Calvin can't stay on that ride for the rest of this life. That he won't be six forever. So instead of cherishing that time, he tries to prepare Calvin to relinquish his wonder, despite the fact that the age of six[1] is nearing the tail end of that childhood magic, anyway. The tragedy of this kind of '80s dad is that the world will be there when the kid is ready to join it. The world isn't going anywhere. Its lessons will come, you don't need to pre-empt them; all you're doing is spoiling the time we have.

This is why, in my mind, the most poignant comic of *Calvin and Hobbes*, as it pertains to dad bods, is the Sunday strip without words that shows Calvin and his dad playing in the snow. Calvin wants to go outside and play. He's all done up in his snowsuit. He asks his dad to join him. Calvin's Dad, a patent lawyer, is doing paperwork. He shrugs, hands open, indicating the work. Sadly, Calvin walks away and goes outside. Calvin's Dad looks out the window at Calvin playing by himself. He looks down at the paperwork. He asks himself, "What am I doing?" then he kits up, goes outside, and joins his son — to Calvin's evident glee. Then, along comes nighttime, and Calvin's Mom holds a pyjamaed boy up for a kiss, and Calvin's Dad works on into the night.

This is real. This is the kind of sacrifice we're talking about, here, that make a man into a father. And yet, it's important to note that this perspective is entirely from the dad's point of

1. Bluey's exact age, by the way.

view, unlike the vast majority of *Calvin and Hobbes*. The normal framing of the strip had to shift in order to accommodate this harmony, which is an earmark for what we already know: this was a special, rare moment for them. This was not business as usual. This was not Calvin's Dad's initial instinct. This was unique, which is even more heart-rending.

The fun of a dad bod like Calvin's Dad is that he does play games, but they're all dad-games, not collaborative games. What that means is that Calvin's Dad is applying a unilateral model of control: he is placing himself above his son, asserting his authority frequently, albeit subtly, and placing distance between himself and Calvin. He introduces paradoxes to Calvin because he thinks they're neat, unaware of the fact that it keeps Calvin up at night. He delegitimizes Calvin's imaginary worries and fears about monsters under the bed and his stuffed tiger, Hobbes.

It pains me to say so, but Calvin's Dad consistently undermines the emotional reality of his son. He believes that his role is to act as an avatar of the superego, which places him on the outside of his son's emotional life, rather than the inside. When confronted by the problem of "We have to go out the door in five minutes and my son is pretending to be a frog," instead of coming up with a fun, creative way to get that froggy out the door, Calvin's Dad says, "No. You're not."

Calvin's Dad is a flawed father figure, but he is still way more real than the others. He is a product of his times in ways that I was not at all aware of until I got neck-deep into my analysis of *Bluey*.

When I think about the tendencies I have toward the kind of dad I don't want to be, while they don't directly come from Calvin's Dad, they do stem from that mindset of superiority and differentiation that places a child's needs and sense of reality somehow inferior to an adult's. It's seductive because it seems more efficient, and because, sure, there are lots of things that kids don't know and you have to keep an eye on them or they'll run into traffic.

That's not what I'm talking about, though. And I'm not convinced that leaning into a power struggle against your kid *in general* is more efficient. My wife and I have had way more success using the weird[1] models of behaviour and parenting techniques that have come out of recent books that all emphasize the value of building up a child's sense of emotional well-being, confirming their lived experience, and connecting with them first and foremost, before you try to redirect their attention toward what you need them to do, or away from whatever you don't want them to do, or try to teach them a lesson. Connecting comes first, and the acid test is indicators from body language that *they* feel like you're listening, that *they* feel respected, that *they* are valued and understood. It centres parenting on the child, and it is kind of nuts, now that I type that out, how much of a Copernican Revolution that is when I compare it to the obedience-centred models from the near-past.

So no, entering into a twenty-year-long power struggle where your experience trumps your child's and your word is the final say that they must obey — I don't think that's more efficient, or effective. It's just lazier.

It seems odd to be calling out Calvin's Dad for laziness, given his explicit emphasis on building character and hard work, and his constant dictum for Calvin to get off the couch and play outside. But the medium doesn't fit the message, because, when I imagine Calvin's Dad, the picture in my head is of a guy sitting in his easy chair, reading a book. He treats that me-time as though it is his due, and primarily seems to be redirecting Calvin away from activities that would disrupt his recreation.

---

1. Or at the very least, unintuitive.

Compared to Bandit, who is right up in there at six in the morning, making breakfasts, playing games, loading the girls up in the wagon to go to the playground, dispensing creative solutions, mediating conflict, playing through role plays that demand *to the hilt* commitment — yeah, it's fair to say that Calvin's Dad is lazy in comparison to our new-model dad bod.

The times where Bandit's ostensibly failing, when he's trying to distract Bluey and Bingo rather than join in with them, or when he wants to just read the newspaper so he tells them to play quietly, over there, don't bother me; when he is being simply assertive without providing a reason for the kids to understand his motivation and their place within it; when he's tired and grumpy, when he's had a bad day, when he finds a cold stone of disengagement or disconnection from his children that he must overcome in order to be the kind of dad he wants to be; when he is overly concerned about the status quo or what other people think or being on time or the general gestalt of the superego — those times when Bandit lets us or them down, that's standard operating procedure for Calvin's Dad, the model of fatherhood that preceded us, and the cluster of associations and assumptions we attribute to dad bods[1] that we, too, must overcome.

Like all of us, he's been humbled by a dog.

---

1. The insecurity that prompts us to take ourselves too seriously.

PART FIVE:
The End

Die, Die-Hard, or the *Die Hard* Dilemma

DIE HARD IS THE ANTI-*ODYSSEY*. The *Odyssey* gives us a kind of ur–dad bod: it paints the picture of the father as the local representative of the society, outlines the calamity that occurs when the patriarch is not present, sets up the mirror of father and political ruler, and shows the outrageous lengths dads will go to when they are separated from their families as Odysseus hops from island to island overcoming any number of mythical foes and situations for ten years. Dad coming home reasserts the status quo, and establishes a core example of Joseph Campbell's Hero's Journey.

In *Die Hard*, a movie about a lone man trapped in a skyscraper with terrorists,[1] you really only have the latter. John McClane (played immaculately by then-newcomer Bruce Willis) is fighting for his life, but he's also fighting for his wife, who is an executive at the Nakatomi Corporation and one of the hostages captured during the corporate Christmas party.

---

1. Who are really high-class thieves posing as terrorists.

It's an inverted *Odyssey*. The time frame is collapsed into a single night. The protagonist holds no special position in society and, from all outward appearances, his family is doing just fine without him. Suitors exist,[1] but are easily rebuffed by McClane's badass wife, Holly (played by Bonnie Bedelia). There is a perceived disruption to the status quo, but it is largely McClane's consternation that his wife is a capable individual, rather than the feeling that the natural world is coming apart at the seams because Dad's not home, which is absolutely the vibe in the *Odyssey*.

What's more, the journey in *Die Hard* is far more obscure than in Homer's epic. McClane doesn't know that he's going on a journey, for starters. For seconders, it is an internal journey, one that is compelled or initiated by the external events (the pain and suffering, the anxiety and tension, the tremendous fear McClane endures and the horrors that he experiences as his identity as a police officer is stripped away through necessity to reveal the cowboy beneath), and instead of arriving at home, he arrives at a revelation: the suitors didn't destroy his home, he did.

It took ego-death to grant McClane the ability to apologize. It took the assumption that he would not survive this night for him to dig out of his soul the shards of understanding that cut even more keenly than the glass embedded in his feet. That's how strong the male identity is. Were it not for this particular cocktail of suspense and adrenaline, plus the fact that McClane escaped death just enough times to realize he didn't have another roll of the Grim Reaper's dice in him, he would never admit fault.

He is so insecure. So unable to listen. So bound to an irrelevant decorum, that upon seeing his beautiful wife after *months* of estrangement, the very first thing he does is leap,

---

1. Poor Ellis.

bare feet first, back into the argument that they had when she decided to take this incredible job opportunity and move from New York to California.

This is what is ticking beneath Bruce Willis's manic terror as he dodges gunfire and tosses bombs down elevator shafts — that he fucked it up with his wife, and now they were going to die terrible, absurd deaths and leave their children orphans in an uncaring America.

The terrorists are symbolic manifestations of the impossibility for the traditionally coded male ego to admit fault. The terrorist leader, Hans Gruber (one of the greatest villains in cinema history, played by another then-newcomer, the late[1] Alan Rickman) is just as much a manifestation of this insecurity as McClane, albeit in a totally different register. Gruber is a living plan. He's a human kanban board, project managing each element of this intricate heist. His goals and motivations are simple, direct, and clean. Like any professional road map, the complexity lives in the details and the doing. When his plan is threatened, Gruber lashes out like a snarling yeti, before becoming one with the plan.

McClane, on the other hand, starts with a set of rules, a code. He is forced to improvise as he sheds that code due to stark pragmatism as it turns out that you can't use police interrogation methods on a pack of thugs with machines guns, C-4, and hostages. As I noted above, he sheds the false identity of the police officer and dons the active identity of the cowboy, living an individual code of justice in a space with no overarching law.

Both of them so desperately desire to be *right*, and their methodologies for defining and producing what is right are so opposed, that they cannot allow one another to exist. They

---

1. Great.

are perfect nemeses for one another. Where McClane is down to earth, alone, fighting for his heart, and improvising his way through the night, Gruber is refined, a leader, operating cerebrally, and driven by a clear set of ambitions mapped to a strict agenda. Yet both of them chafe at Holly's persistent insistence that they did not think about the entire picture, that they simply aren't objectively correct, that their perception of themselves and the world is inaccurate. Neither of them can handle it.

As much as the superficial plot layers of *Die Hard* are the kind of beautiful machinery of a Swiss watch — each scene building to the next, each beat timed to perfection, each increase in tension met with a form of catharsis that complicates and pushes the film to its thrilling, perfect, holiday-themed, jokey but dead serious, cowboy-trickster duel — as delightful as that cake of cinema cuts, it is the layer just beneath symbolism that cuts me right back: the dad becomes reintegrated with his family at the end, and yes, all becomes right in the world.

.

As a character, John McClane has a very similar fate as John Rambo. Both present the unique idea of a vulnerable action hero, who is played with fear, anxiety, and mental instability at the forefront of their performances. Especially Willis, who is driven to such extremes by the events that he witnesses and participates in that you can hear the cables of his mental fibre fraying with each brief, expletive-laden soliloquy. The humanity of that character speaks so much louder than the action set pieces that kept the meat glued to the seat.

However, it also makes these Johns tragic, because with each improbable, tacked-on sequel the characters are flattened, made that much more cartoonish, until they enter a state of self-parody. Later *Rambo* movies became so horrifically violent because they forgot that there was any other component to this poor Vietnam vet. They were bleached away by the dollarbucks piled up in Stallone's swimming pool. What the hell does a Vietnam vet mean in 2008 or 2019, anyway? Meanwhile, the last ten *Die Hard* movies feature an ever-shinier-skulled Willis punching jets and arm-wrestling helicopters, combatting villains with schemes pulled from comic books rather than paperbacks.

The great failure of these franchises was making more than one movie.

It reminds me of a totally wild interview you can find online of Bruce Willis, Sylvester Stallone, and Arnold Schwarzenegger on a British talk show, right around the time they were promoting Planet Hollywood, the costume-and-prop-themed family-friendly restaurant franchise. I was initially blown away by the idea of these three leading action men of the '80s/'90s sharing a stage on a talk show, and realized that this could only have occurred in the British Isles. Their publicists would never let them be seen as anything other than individuals stateside, as collaboration among leading men was anathema to their existence until postmodernism gave us a reboot of *Ocean's Eleven* and nostalgia-driven action old folks' homes like *The Expendables*.

The second thing that blew me away was a revelation from Bruce Willis. All the other guys were ribbing him about how much he got paid to play John McClane in the third *Die Hard* instalment: *Die Hard with a Vengeance*. Bruce was visibly uncomfortable, so the polite British talk show host cut to a trailer of Bruce's next film, a trifle about a cop with a boat called *Striking Distance*. After the clip was played, Bruce Willis looked physically ill, and the host said, "Another cop. What's the appeal with cops over there?"

Bruce Willis said that they were starting to lose their appeal for him and he was "getting sick of carrying guns in movies."

He tried to justify it by saying that these were the modern generation's cowboy movies, the endless need for good guys and bad guys. Then his voice cracked and dropped a register. "I just get a little tired of all the guns, after a while."[1]

All the way back in 1993, Bruce Willis was done with guns.[2] As a kid raised on a diet of *Die Hard* this was as crushing as it was fascinating. As a father trying to figure out how the heck to help my son navigate the awesome[3] violence inherent in traditionally male-coded identity and riven throughout our cultural products, I can't help but find a great deal of sympathy for Bruce's unheard plea on British television.

Audiences just can't get enough of Bruce Willis's left-handed pistol stylings, and *Die Hard* was the movie that started it all.

•

He said it, that lone plea to escape his successful movie persona, with the same sincere fear McClane has when he knows his death is upon him, and he will never see his wife and kids again. Never be able to repair the wounds that he has caused them. Never be able to overcome the limitations of an old-fashioned form of masculinity that both informs and shackles him in this ever-changing world. He will never be

---

1. The conversation then slid to Schwarzenegger and Stallone, who had been sitting there, politely smiling the entire time. The host asked them about James Bond and the tradition of action movies with one-liners. Arnold gave a totally slick, totally pro, PR-friendly answer about how Bond is the action hero that has it all: humour, entertainment, great action, larger-than-life plots. He loved it (well, the Sean Connery and Roger Moore ones, anyway). Stallone ran for a bit with a really cogent analysis on the value of humour in a violent movie to add to its escapist nature, saying that jokes relieve the audience of the tension of watching violence and help them recognize that this isn't something to take seriously, and he called it a feature of the '90s, which I find interesting.

2. But guns weren't done with Bruce. Since then, he's been featured in fifty-one films predicated on the gratuitous use of firearms.

3. I mean that biblically.

able to grow into the man he might become, if only he could live free, rather than die hard.

.

The *Die Hard* Dad bod is the one I identify with the most. I have made a lot of mistakes, in my life and my relationship with my wife, as a father and an individual. I live in fear of what I won't be able to do, whether it's due to the circumstances around me — the terrorists of time that must be dealt with but provide no avenue to understanding — or the limitations that come from within, that are part and parcel of the models I have imbibed to make me who and what I am.

Unlike John McClane, I cannot yank those shards of glass from my feet, because I cannot tell the difference between the feet and the wounds.

I also have a very hard time admitting fault, and tend to see disagreement in terms of a power struggle, whether I want to or not.

I am terrified of the things I won't be able to tell my friends and family, or of the lack of courage to confront the fears that get in the way of me living a life of true joy and deep harmony.

I fear that I will allow my need for control[1] to control me, driving me further and further from the present moment, utterly unable to reconcile and connect, to integrate with those around me because I will forever be frozen in the paralysis of fear that comes from the possibility of making a mistake.

I fear authority. I fear failing it, I fear having it, I fear abusing it, I fear being abused by it. I fear being put in an unfair position to prove that I have what it takes, because I know that I don't, or else I wouldn't have this pervasive sense of dread.

---

1. A false panacea to mitigate the fear.

I fear being found out and shown to be the clown and fraud that I, deep down, know myself to be.

I fear ... being a bad dad.

The *Die Hard* Dad bod is fuelled by fear and insecurity, trapped in a nightmare, hunted by terrorists, utterly ill-equipped to deal with the situation that he's fallen into. (The poor bastard doesn't even have any shoes.) That fear, that situation of feeling insecure, that sense of being hunted and haunted, trapped within a construct that also defines you — that's the core of all of the dad bods we have explored so far.

That, my friends, is the most likely candidate for what it means to be a man.

To transcend and eclipse this blood moon of self-gnawing identity demands a recalibration both within and without, a support structure of family and friends you can be honest and open with, but also a set of role models both independent of these social conditions as well as utterly, utterly embedded within them.

Embedded within these mores, but not defined by them.

To act as a bridge between all this toxic junk and another way.

Down for the Count

I WANT TO TALK ABOUT one scene in *Dracula*, smack dab in the middle of Bram Stoker's legendary vampire novel. In it, the Count is in the process of seducing the main female character, Mina, and transforming her into a vampire — a long process that rolls out like a disease, a mysterious illness that slowly saps health and will from our erstwhile hero. Despite the fact that Mina is protected by a brace of tall, handsome leading men ranging from sea captains to Texans to Van Helsing (an actual vampire hunter), night after night Dracula continues courting her.

In a way, this night monster is framed as a rapacious teenage boy, slipping past this cordon of dads who have taken it upon their Victorian selves to act as shield and bulwark against the psychic, sexual, and mystical advances of our aristocratic villain.

To call the Count a "teenage boy" does not give him enough credit, though. He outfoxes all of Mina's protectors because he is an experienced, patient predator. He knows when to lie in wait, when to approach, and when to let his minions do the work. He leaves little to chance, and strikes when the iron is hot. No addle-brained, gangly-armed, hormone-inflated monster is he, oh no, he's a pro.

He is also, literally and figuratively, a monster. That hyper-predatory nature is represented in the shape-shifting forms that the Count takes: a massive wolf-dog, a horrendous bat, and a kind of sentient mist that can slip through even a crack as razor-thin as the lid of a tomb. Each of these forms is a tool for gaining entry to where he isn't wanted. So too is this hyper-predatory nature lurking in the Count's drive and motivations: there is no man he does not wish to best, no woman he does not wish to conquer — or, better yet, hypnotically enslave their mind so they *beg him to* conquer them.

As a member of the aristocracy, dominance is as natural for the Count as breathing is for us.

He codes as hypermasculine.

In the scene I want to discuss, Mina is partway through her transformation into a vampire. Her blood is thinning, so the men protecting her give her regular transfusions of their own, to help satiate her ravenous hunger and, they hope, draw her away from the Count's control. Each night she sleeps a terrible sleep, guarded by these men who, despite being very raw and macho, are no match for the Count, shackled as they are by their humanity.

That night, the party of male protectors bursts into Mina's room when they hear a sound. There they find her, bent over the Count. He's kneeling in her bed, topless, and he's opened up a gash in his chest from which Mina's slurping. His hand is clutching her head, pulling her into this embrace, shoving her mouth into his wet wound.

If you read the scene sexually,[1] then Dracula is both forcing oral sex *and nursing her* from his demonic teat, as he symbolically gives birth to another vampire in his brood.

---

1. And how *can't* you? The whole book is an incredible, multi-layered and multi-textured investigation into Victorian sexual fears lashed at the waist to a badass monster horror adventure.

Now the hypermale has horseshoed, gone so far down the trail, beyond the conventions and assumptions of normal Victorian society's gender codes that he has turned them into an ouroboros. He is a dark mother, a hypermasculine predator, a seducer who unlocks women's "evil" libidinous nature, and the taunting Freudian father to the pack of vampire hunters, saying, "Come on, take me if you can."

Count Dracula is all, simultaneously; a mouth full of sharp fangs of identity that complicate and drive each other in a single bite.

Taken as a whole, reread with this scene in mind, the novel perpetuates an incredibly dense antagonist who scoffs at the categories we might attempt to place upon him.

This is one way out of the *Die Hard* Dad dilemma — that raging traditional male need to be perceived as masculine, and the resulting cascade of insecure, doubling-down, adamant aversion to change.

·

As rich and loamy source material, *Dracula* is like the soil from home that the Count stuffs into his coffin to cross the sea and remain in vital spirits. Despite attempts to rewrite much of the lore surrounding the character, *Castlevania* can't help but carry the weight and meaning of that fertile groundwork. Dracula is bigger than *Castlevania*, and so his conceptual power tugs the video game and anime franchise along on a string, like any pretty fool caught in a vampire's gaze.

As a villain for the Belmont family to fight *forever*, Dracula is perfect. Dracula is forever an outsider. He lives above human morality, beyond the apparatus of the state to confine, and between worlds of conventional identity. This is most obviously coded in sexuality, as the Count is a complicated meditation on queerness, individuality, and power.

However, I belong to that bastard generation that experienced countless postmodern pastiches before I was of an age to root out the source material. So, despite the obvious referential power of using a figure like Dracula in your video game,[1] for me the nostalgia and drive of engagement is clearly set in reverse.

I need to buck *Castlevania* from my mind when I read *Dracula*, lest I approach the primary work as an offshoot instead of an antecedent.

⁕

That feeling of doing surgery upon myself, to extract the fundamental childhood imaginary that established my understanding of vampires in the first place is, to be frank, a big part of why I want to talk about *Castlevania*.

It's what dads need to do in order to transcend the limitations of our blinkered definition of masculinity.

⁕

One of my favourite essays of all time describes Stoker's achievement as transforming the vampire story into "an ongoing referendum on the philosophy of Friedrich Nietzsche."[2] On the

---

1. Which, when you think about really old games like the original *Castlevania*, have to function like haiku — supremely direct because the expressive power of the format is stunningly truncated. So of course this limited medium would lean on previous associations of narrative structure, such as the princess-rescue, or content, like recycling well-known archetypes and figures in the public domain, a feature of video game design that has become so fetishized that, despite gargantuan leaps in mimesis, the vast majority of characters in video games wear their tropes like an old coat.

2. Christian Thorne, "Staying Alive: Part One," August 18, 2011, found on his website, hosted by Williams University, sites.williams.edu/cthorne/articles/staying-alive-part-one/.

exploration of a morality that goes beyond the common, shared human etiquette. On individuals who create their own values.

•

Dracula is as manly as they come. He is also a gender-bending creature of the night. This terrifies the protagonists of the story, each and every one reeling from the revaluation of sexuality and gender, power and self that Dracula forces them to consider.

Dracula is having a good time, and these square-jawed straight guys can't handle it.

•

Now, it goes without saying that the predatory manifestation of masculinity that so cruelly and centrally pumps through Dracula's hollow demonic bosom is not what I'm talking about. I'm thinking about the form, not the content. The idea that one can inhabit multiple seemingly contradictory identity spaces simultaneously when one abandons the fear of conformity and sees oneself as an entity that strides between codes of conduct — dads need to practise that code-switching, whether or not they want to dabble in gender-bending.

It's useful, period, because it frees one from the shackles of previous association, and if having a kid is going to do anything, it is going to demand that you grow beyond your limitations.

•

Not to "become" a father, in the sense of just applying a new mask and a new set of rules to your figure. That's only the most superficial reading of these texts and falls into the trap of inhabiting the symbol rather than consciously utilizing it. If you "become" a father this way, grafting it to a new set of definitions, then you haven't really grown at all, and you certainly haven't grown free of the fear that nestles like a snake at the root of dad bods.

You've just switched rooms in the prison.

•

If there is a way, it can't be delineated. Then it's just another net. Another noose. If you go down that trail then you'll end up like the father at the end of *The Road*, without purpose and without substance as soon as your child doesn't need you. A shambling skeleton who drops dead upon the cessation of the terminally defined quest to get this kid into adulthood.

•

No, what I mean is growing beyond the need for definitions, and thus growing beyond the rubric of dad bods. To take the shape of the context you're in, and find the freedom to be whatever is needed — to see that being in the form of a dance, a shift from man to wolfhound to mist. From dad to partner to what you are when you're alone, in the dark, looking in a mirror at the brimming emptiness behind your eyes.

•

It's no easy task, to try to take a hard look at the experiences and messages that inform your perception and biases. It's damned painful, for one thing, and it's impossible to do cleanly, given that the apparatus of your inspection is also a part of what you're trying to inspect.

It's a bit like trying to bite your own teeth.

Of course, others can help, but like many practices of growth or self-development, the individual under the knife needs to consent. Otherwise, the project will be doomed from the start, trapped in the hangar. If you can't hear what your heart is telling you, if you aren't open to the possibility of being surprised, if you don't see the portcullis as a concern — then you can live inside Joseph Campbell's castle.

The rest must step outside, and go beyond the walls they were raised within.

.

A father is a symbol. A role one must play in order to establish a tiny human in the world. Once the symbol has served its purpose, feel free to toss it aside. It is a role one must wear, but not inhabit.

Otherwise, it is a trap and a burden, and one that dads inadvertently place on their children as soon as they grow beyond needing someone to hold their hand and tell them what to do.

So many dads cling to that role far after its best-before date, and suffer the inevitable fallout of a loss of purpose — or else they cling assiduously to the role and become filled with resentment as it is no longer heeded.

What's more, it is impossible to be that symbol. To hold yourself to the standards of how a child sees you will never work out.

Unless you can do so consciously, in happy expectation of dropping the mask at a later date when your kid grows up and becomes self-sufficient.[1] Then you can eschew the need for a symbol-draped persona and just be a person with them.

If, on the other hand, you unconsciously graft this sense of fatherhood onto your identity and self-definition, then you will cling to it as tightly as the day is long. This not only prohibits your kid from growing up[2] (and not needing you as protector and symbol of the wider net of society's mores), but also

---

1. Or simply sees through the charade.

2. Or, rather, forces them to grow up in opposition to the role you're playing.

prohibits *you* from growing up and getting the opportunity to realize a self beyond this rigid symbolic role play.

•

Something adjacent to this "going beyond" is needed of dads who wish to define themselves as men. To go beyond the frail and winnowed role of orthodox or toxic masculinity. To go beyond the fears that are so threaded through our identity that they have replaced the full spectrum of the nervous system. To go beyond our limited selves and find a new way to be … Constantly becoming.

A Dad Becoming

WHEN I WAS YOUNGER, I used to need to know the end before I could begin doing something. If I couldn't figure it all out before the first step, I was paralyzed by indecision.

I'm still working on that.

.

(I want to be able to improvise. To step across stones in the river of life and have justifiable faith that I will be able to determine or create a way to the other side.)

.

When I dressed my son for the first time, in a little lion sleeper, I was ready for anything. I had no idea where our family would go, what we would do, or who he would become.

I still don't. He's only two.

.

Between these two stances lies a gulf I cannot connect. It feels asinine to sum them up as fear and love, but the analysis holds no matter how I slice it.

My love for my son is transformational. It may be subtle, and I may be the same knucklehead, but I am also in the throes of this transformation. So too is this book.

What started out as a book of arguments became, organically, step by step, a travelogue of an inward journey through the media that made me. That makes me.

·

Any conclusion before death is provisional at best.

·

It's weird, writing a book of essays about burgeoning fatherhood and representations of dads in the media, while also being hyper-aware of the fact that I am barely a father and as far away from lucid as I've ever been in my life.

Perhaps it's important to note that I am neither a full-time writer nor an independently wealthy person. I have a day job. It would be nice to be hella transparent about how stupid difficult it is to try to create a meaningful work of art when I am absolutely gripped by my emotional connection to my son. Like Fay Wray in *King Kong*, I'm carried around by a force so powerful and gargantuan that I cannot comprehend it.

This one weekend in late July, my wife, son, and I were invited out to a cottage her parents were house-sitting for family friends. At this time, I was straight-up panicking because a deadline from my (lovely) publishers was only six weeks away. Writing is slow business at the best of times, and my process with this book has been weird and all over the place. Heaps of research notes. Tons of dead ends. Watching movies and playing games takes *time*, man. I was also about halfway through the probationary period for a new, very intense, very promising job.

Plus we had spent lots of bandwidth on domestic, time-eating tasks recently (we moved out of Toronto, we'd just finished potty training our son, we were trying to find a new daycare, not to mention the constant mental-health judo[1] of the pandemic) and I was still doing my old job of part-time consulting because I cared/believed in the client and wanted them to succeed and this was a pivotal time in their organization.

Long story short, there hadn't been very much quiet time for concentrating.

So my wife proposed that she go to see her family with our son and I have half a weekend to myself to work on "the book."[2]

That was a very lovely, very generous offer.

Nonetheless, it felt so wrong. We tried to go through with it, but, in the end, I couldn't pull the trigger.

This is a book about dads and dadhood. It felt grotesque to try to sequester its creation from my real, messy life of being a dad. So instead, we incorporated it. As my son and wife played in the lake with my in-laws, I sat perched above, doing what I could with Gandalf and Bandit, and stepping down to play with them when the gravity well in my heart tugged too heavily.

It feels right if this book is a product of this stage of my life and development. What that means is I wrote this in bursts, both of time and clarity, that occurred between the yells and the accidental pees, the meals that ended up all over the floor, the incredible growth and learning, and the daily reminder that life is change.

Rather than a refined gem, this whole project is a bit of a cabochon.

But it is also an organic artistic expression of fatherhood, coming out of the crucible of a real life with just as many responsibilities and time-sinks as I could possibly imagine.

---

1. Aikido?

2. That's what we call it, as though it is the only book in our life. I'm reminded of Thomas Aquinas's "Hominem unius libri timeo."

Not to mention the sleep deprivation.[1]

The paradox of being a dad writer who is writing a book about fatherhood is that it makes me incredibly emotional and want to spend more time with my son. Two and a half is a very special age. The whole world is magic. I cannot countenance taking even more time away from him than I have to in order to make a living. It's unconscionable, which is a word I've never said out loud.

To that end, I've taken to writing this book whenever he is asleep: either during nap time on the weekends, before he wakes up in the mornings (when it's a gamble that I'll even be cogent, let alone lucid), or (like now, as I write these final words) late at night, pushing up against the morrow.

Hence the *Tristram Shandy* quote at the beginning. The structure that grew out of this is different from my initial intention. I wanted a string of polished, multi-faceted gems that you could read and reread over and over to gather new meaning on the many angles of inference that these models of fatherhood, these tropes, archetypes, and symbol-clusters manifested through a new conceptual vocabulary that I tinkered together with precision and refinement. Instead, no, I'm like Tristram Shandy himself. These ideas and perspectives grew and grew over the two years I worked on this book, and these dads started talking to one another, here in the echoey room of my head. The essays became bundles, the notions interleaved, and the writing far more naturalistic (as in, written more like an email than a poem) due to the fact that I punched some of this out while my son was talking to me about his stuffed tiger[2] and we were looking out the window at his cousins being pulled on an

---

1. Have I mentioned you never sleep again, once you become a parent?

2. "Blondie," a Hobbes-sized stuffy we picked up at IKEA as a, let's say, "compromise," when a certain someone didn't want to leave the toy section.

inflatable manta ray behind a boat. I don't have a day to test the prosody of each sentence with a tuning fork. And even if I did, I wouldn't want it.

That wouldn't reflect the realities of this project.

That wouldn't be a dad's bod.

I don't have the bandwidth, as an artist, to stare in the mirror and curl barbells of vocabulary. I've got to go make dinner. Or I've got to go to bed. Or I have work in an hour, and my wife and son are asleep in our bed after he crawled in there at four in the morning because the "scary black balls" that "move" are in his room again, and he tried to keep his toes warm in my armpit.

That's the kind of book this is.[1]

·

I think I've said enough for now, perhaps too much.

Good night.

---

1. I hope you enjoyed it.

Acknowledgements

A BOOK IS A THING with one person's name on the front despite being the product of countless individuals' contributions. *Dad Bod* was created in conversation. My thoughts about these movies, shows, and video games are just dreaming in an empty room. None of this would have been possible without years of mouthing off with too many people to count. Anyone who's talked to me about art: thank you.

To my friends. First off, thank you, Jan W. Streekstra, for two years of riffing on dad bods and thirty-four years of friendship. *Nec tamen consumebatur.* Thank you, Sean, Leor, Dustin (and Mike), there's nobody else I'd rather ponder orbs with. Thank you, Tim and Steve, Mimi and Derek, André, Liz, and Simon. You all helped me not give up, in one way or another. Thank you, Emily M. Keeler, for publishing my first essay a decade ago. I miss our walks out to the Distillery District. Thank you, Charles Yao, for so, so many things over the years, but most of all your sense of humour.

To the mentors, whether or not they knew it. Thank you, David Lavin, for teaching me how to sell ideas. Thank you, Blaine Allan, for teaching me how to think about film. Thank you, Adele Mercier, for teaching me how to think. Thank you, Mark McKechnie, I still have the postcard.

To my publisher. Let's start with my editor, Julie Mannell, without whom there would be no *Dad Bod*, thank you for telling me exactly what I needed to do, exactly how I needed to hear it. Thank you, Jess Shulman, for being an incredible whetstone. And thank you, Jenny McWha, Laura Boyle, Erin Pinksen, Alyssa Boyden, and everyone else at Dundurn for making this book a reality.

To my family, thank you for believing in me and loving me and for seeing in me the kind of person I can become. Mom and Dad, as parents and examples of parenting, I don't have the words to thank you enough. Mel, thank you for your wit. Ron and Ev, thank you for accepting me. Cheryl, Chris, Em, and Al, thank you for standing in minus twenty degrees Celcius to watch *Die Hard* with me.

L—: thank you for being my son. All of the meaningful words are because of you.

Last, but certainly not least, thank you, Jenn. For choosing me every day, and making me a father.

About the Author

CIAN CRUISE WAS BORN IN Kingston, Ontario, and attended Queen's University, where he studied philosophy and film. He then moved to Toronto and worked in advertising, marketing, and sales before becoming a freelance writer and consultant. His cultural criticism has appeared in *Hazlitt*, *Maisonneuve*, *Playboy*, *Vulture*, and *Little Brother Magazine*. Cian lives in Almonte, Ontario, with his family.